THE ETHICS OF TORTURE

J. JEREMY WISNEWSKI AND R. D. EMERICK

continuum

Continuum International Publishing Group

The Tower Building	80 Maiden Lane
11 York Road	Suite 704
London SE1 7NX	New York, NY 10038

www.continuumbooks.com

British Library Cataloguing-in-Publication Data
A catalogue record for this book is available from the British Library.

ISBN-10: HB: 0-8264-9889-2
PB: 0-8264-9890-6
ISBN-13: HB: 978-0-8264-9889-2
PB: 978-0-8264-9890-8

Library of Congress Cataloging-in-Publication Data
Wisnewski, Jeremy.
The ethics of torture / J. Jeremy Wisnewski and R. D. Emerick.
p. cm.
Includes bibliographical references.
ISBN-13: 978-0-8264-9889-2 (HB)
ISBN-13: 978-0-8264-9890-8 (pbk.)
ISBN-10: 0-8264-9889-2 (HB)
ISBN-10: 0-8264-9890-6 (pbk.)
1. Torture–Moral and ethical aspects. I. Emerick, R. D. II. Title.

HV8593.W57 2009
172'.2–dc22

2008043687

Typeset by Newgen Imaging Systems Pvt Ltd, Chennai, India
Printed and bound in Great Britain by MPG Books Ltd, Bodmin,
Cornwall

To those who have survived, and
to those who could not

CONTENTS

ACKNOWLEDGMENTS

The authors would like to thank the numerous people who have endured their interest in this dark subject over the years. Several people have contributed to the development of the ideas contained in this book. In general, audiences at various conferences have offered engaging and lively commentary and criticism which have vastly improved the arguments put forth in this text. Material has been presented at sessions sponsored by the Society for Philosophy in the Contemporary World (SPCW) on Torture at both the 2004 Eastern Division APA, as well as a 2007 session at the Pacific Division APA; material has also been presented at Hartwick College under various guises (including a presentation as part of the 2007–2008 Faculty Lecture Series), at the University of Colorado at Denver, at the 2008 Conference of the Athens Institute for Research and Education, in Athens, Greece, and at the 2008 Meeting of the SPCW in Snow Mountain Ranch, Colorado; work-in-progress was also presented to the "Habermas and Violence" Panel at the Political Theory Workshops, Fourth Annual Conference, held at Manchester Metropolitan University, 2007. While we would like to thank everyone in attendance at these venues, many people deserve special thanks for their insightful remarks and encouraging criticism. These people include: Stanley Konecky, Ed Grippe, Aaron Lercher, Janet Donohoe, Andrew Fiala, Jose-Antonio Orosco, David Hildebrand, Rob Metcalf, Candice Shelby, Wanda Teays, and Jean Maria Arrigo. Thanks also go to students who took courses with J. Jeremy Wisnewski on the topic of torture, or who have otherwise assisted with the development of this manuscript. Particular thanks go to Meg Lonergan and Josh Simmonds.

We would also like to thank the following publications for permission to reprint previously published material. Thanks go to the *Journal of Social Philosophy* for permission to reprint

"Unwarranted Torture Warrants: A Critique of the Dershowitz Proposal," which originally appeared in Volume 39, Number 2, Summer 2008. Thanks are also due to the *International Journal of Applied Philosophy,* for permission to reprint "It's About Time: Defusing the Ticking Bomb Argument," which first appeared in Volume 22, Number 1, 2008.

The writing of this manuscript was supported by a Faculty Research Grant generously provided by Hartwick College in 2007–2008 and 2008–2009.

A project such as this could not have been completed without the support and love of our families. We thus wish to thank our wives, Dorothy and Victoria, as well as our daughters, Audrey and Lilia, for reminding us of all that's good in the world.

CHAPTER ONE

COMING TO (DEFINITIONAL) TERMS WITH TORTURE

FOUR MODELS

The attempt to define torture has been hopeless. There have been several attempts at defining the term, but none have been particularly effective. In some cases, these attempts have been motivated by the far-from-disinterested agendas of those doing the defining. In other cases, the issue has centered more on the problem of the term itself: torture, from the Latin *tortura,* originally meaning to turn or twist. The thing described—or rather, the many things described—have been a part of robust judicial proceedings, evidence gathering, state witch-hunts, psychotic fetishes, and religious crusades. There is no chapter of human history that is without it.

While it will be worth exploring (briefly) how various attempts at definition have failed adequately to capture certain forms of torture, or have succeeded in blinding us to certain kinds of abuse, it is our contention that there is simply no way to capture all dimensions of torture in a specific definition. This does not entail, however, that we must simply be silent on the issue of the meaning of torture. The key, we think, is to distinguish types of torture (much as we might distinguish types of games). Once we have done this, we are able to say quite a bit about what specific kinds of torture involve. This can be further refined by discussing different models of what torture involves. As we will demonstrate, the sorts of moral issues that arise when investigating torture depend substantially on the hermeneutic horizon one is employing in order to understand the phenomenon in question. It is our view that none of the existing interpretational horizons (no particular models) of torture are significantly more important than others. Each model reveals a particular aspect of the practice of torture, and hence is worthy of investigation.

Our aim in this book is to lay out the most important types and models of torture and reveal, through careful argument and analysis, what each of these models reveal about the moral impermissibility of torture. Perhaps surprisingly, the case of torture can teach us a lot about ourselves as moral agents, and about what is involved in appropriate interactions with one another. Before jumping into the fray, however, it is necessary to take care of some argumentative preliminaries. First, we will have a look at some of those definitions of torture offered, examining their respective failings. This will enable us to articulate several distinct *kinds* of torture. Following this, we will articulate four models of torture that enable us to investigate the practice with more precision. Finally, we will examine some of the positions taken on torture.

DEFINITIONS AND KINDS OF TORTURE
UN Convention against Torture

> *Article One: For the purposes of this Convention, the term "torture" means any act by which severe pain or suffering, whether physical or mental, is intentionally inflicted on a person for such purposes as obtaining from him or a third person information or a confession, punishing him for an act he or a third person has committed or is suspected of having committed, or intimidating or coercing him or a third person, or for any reason based on discrimination of any kind, when such pain or suffering is inflicted by or at the instigation of or with the consent or acquiescence of a public official or other person acting in an official capacity. It does not include pain or suffering arising only from, inherent in, or incidental to lawful sanctions.*

As many commentators have remarked, this definition is hardly satisfactory. The definition covers both too much and too little. The definition covers too much in that certain cases of coercive violence which are clearly *not* torture must be classified as such under this definition. It covers too little in that some seemingly obvious cases of torture (such as that used by the Marquis de Sade, or by a sociopath of a different color) are not covered by the definition. The problem, we think, lies in the attempt to specify one particular thing called "torture," when in fact there is a family of related practices and activities that can be felicitously characterized as "torture." Moreover, the malicious creativity of torture makes it difficult for governmental and political bodies to adequately define it. If some practices are specified as torture (and thus outlawed), determined practitioners will get to work on novel techniques not covered in the definition. So for the sake of policy, treaties, and conventions, it is often better to have a suitably broad definition. This is a double-edged sword, for with broadness comes vagueness, which makes it particularly difficult to police the practice.

Let's examine some of the particular problems present in the UN definition. The first problem to highlight here is a problem of vagueness. The problem here lies in the use of notoriously difficult-to-define terms (such as "severe" in talking about pain). There is simply no good way of elaborating what it is that will count as "severe" mental or physical pain. This, of course, is a common problem with definitions of a great many difficult concepts. By itself, it is not sufficient to reject the definition offered in the UN Convention. It has, however, occasioned some abuse, and hence is worth noting.[1]

An additional problem with the definition is that it insists that torture is carried out by a "public official," or person acting in an "official capacity." Thus, the definition already seems to exclude many instances of torture that ought not to be so excluded: when a person kidnaps and tortures a victim, it seems irrelevant that the torturer is not doing so in an "official capacity," but rather as a private monster. Of course, to be fair to the UN Convention, the definition in question is only meant to apply to those *nations* that ratify the convention. Hence, there is no need to go beyond the realm of those acting in the name of the state, as the treaty only *covers* actions attributable to the representatives of nations agreeing to the treaty. Nevertheless, seeing why the UN definition is ineffective is useful, if only in that it reveals the difficulty in defining a term like "torture."

A third problem is the limited intentions that are permissible under the Convention (though note, again, that these might well be the only kinds of intentions an agent of the state, *qua* agent of the state, can have). There are three kinds of intentions that are mentioned in the definition: (1) to obtain information, (2) to punish, and (3) to coerce. The first two intentions might be distinguished into two kinds of torture: interrogational and punitive (more on this below). The third category, however, seems simply too broad.

Consider: a guard in a prison uses force against an inmate in order to prevent the inmate from attacking a fellow prisoner. In the course of using such force, the inmate breaks his wrist. Under the UN definition, this will count as torture. The guard is an agent of the state, acting in an official capacity. He has inflicted what looks like severe physical pain on a ward of the state, and has done so with the aim of coercing him. Clearly, though, this is not a case of torture in any standard sense. Granted, there are things about the case that are similar to torture. Nevertheless, no one would suggest that the guard in question should be tried for torture. If the guard has overstepped his authority (which he arguably has), it is because his action involved too much force in response to a given threat. This, however, is not simply equivalent to engaging in torture. There are simply too many differences: the prisoner was not completely helpless, the guard was acting in self-defense, and the time in which the pain was inflicted seems far too short.

The above case, of course, relies on certain intuitions about what constitutes torture that not everyone shares. We do not intend the case to *establish* the nature of torture. The point of this intuition pump is to demonstrate some of the difficulties inherent in the UN Convention definition of torture. The definition at least *arguably* covers any coercive violence conducted by agents of the state, and this is far too inclusive.

Other definitions fare no better, and some fare substantially worse. The Bybee Memo, written for Alberto Gonzales while he was counsel to President George W. Bush, claims that torture must involve a certain level of pain, the definition of which strains credulity:

> Physical pain amounting to torture must be equivalent in intensity to the pain accompanying serious physical injury, such as organ failure, impairment of bodily function, or even death. For purely mental pain or suffering to amount to torture . . . it must result in significant psychological harm of

4

significant duration, e.g. lasting for months or even years. (317)[2]

An obvious problem with this attempt at definition is that it is impossible to determine if acts of psychological torture are in fact torture while they are being carried out. As the above definition makes clear, an act that inflicts mental pain or suffering is *only* torture if it *in fact* results in "significant psychological harm" for a "significant duration." The definition *does not* claim that an act will *most likely* result in such harm; rather, the definition claims that some such harm must be the actual result. This entails that an act cannot be torture until months or years after it has occurred. This particular result of the above definition sounds rather like backward causation, and hence demonstrates the serious shortcomings of the definition of torture contained in the Bybee memorandum.

There are, of course, many additional definitions that we might explore. Rather than belaboring the difficulties in defining torture, though, we suggest an alternative strategy. If we wanted to define "game," on seeing that we could not do it at the most general level, we might either (1) give up the enterprise of definition, or (2) aim our inquiry to more specific sub-types of games in order to see what we might discover about our object domain at a greater level of particularity. As is often the case, the higher the level of definitional abstraction, the more difficult the task— and often, interestingly, the less the payoff of our conceptual archaeology. Rather than pursue the definition of "game," one might well pursue definitions of *types* of games: board games, strategy games, card games, ball games etc., acknowledging that there is no (perfectly) unifying account, that there will likely be significant overlap in many of the categories, and that it is only our linguistic and perceptual competence that holds together the divergent elements of the family we are investigating.

It is with this in mind that we will turn our attention to the *kinds* of torture that are most familiar to us, leaving aside the issue of whether or not there is some grand unifying definition underlying them all. Although there are undoubtedly many ways to mark the distinctions in kinds of torture, some more useful than others, we will begin with what we regard as a fairly standard set of types of torture, as outlined below.

KINDS OF TORTURE

- Judicial/Evidential: this form of torture is such that it has become a part of judicial proceedings. Judicial torture was prevalent until the seventeenth century, at which time its existence began to wane.
- Punitive: this is torture as punishment. The "blood sanctions" of the Middle Ages were crimes that resulted in death or maiming (capital crimes). Later, sentences were often commuted to hard labor or galley work. Some of the punishments meted out are easily characterized as "torture," others less so.
- Interrogational: this is torture aimed at acquiring information, such as that which might be useful to law enforcement. When members of the US military defend torture, it is almost always this *kind* of torture that is under discussion: torture aimed at information, *not* at evidence for criminal proceedings. As Henry Shue points out, the purpose of this kind of torture "appears to be consistent with the observation of some constraint on the part of any torturer genuinely pursuing that purpose alone" (53).
- Dehumanizing: this is torture aimed primarily at "breaking" a subject. (The metaphor here is apt, as what is broken cannot be unbroken). This type of torture is aimed at shaming a prisoner—destroying his identity—rather than at obtaining information. The aim of such torture is "to bring about a change in the victim's self-conception" (351).[3]
- Terroristic/Deterrent: this is torture which aims to deter future incidents of certain sorts (e.g. future military operations, insurgencies, etc.). This type of torture obviously can and does overlap with some of the other categories. One aim of punitive torture, after all, might well be to deter future crimes. Likewise, engaging in torture as a means of de-humanizing a person might well have a deterrent effect. Christopher Tindale usefully characterizes this form of torture as follows: "Its aim is to discourage or encourage certain activities on the part of the victim or other people, or perhaps both. Unlike interrogational torture, the victims of deterrent torture may be chosen at random" (351). As Henry Shue notes,

> The victim's suffering . . . is being used entirely as a means to an end over which the victim has no control.

> Terroristic torture is a pure case—the purest possible case—of the violation of the Kantian principle that no person may be used *only* as a means. . . . (53)[4]

- Sadistic: this is torture undertaken for the sheer joy of it, as seen, for example, in some of the fictional work of the Marquis de Sade.

Obviously, what we will have to say in the pages that follow will have a bearing on *all* forms of torture, as we will argue that torture of any kind is morally impermissible. Nevertheless, certain forms of torture will be the focus of our discussion, while other forms will scarcely be mentioned. Torture as sadism, for example, will receive little treatment in what follows. This is not because there is nothing of interest psychologically and philosophically in such cases. It is rather because there are *no* persons who actively defend non-consensual sadism as a *moral* enterprise. Indeed, part of Sade's fascination with torturous sexual practices is that it defies all morality. As such, sadistic torture will receive little treatment. Likewise, we will not spend any substantial amount of time considering punitive torture, as this is advocated by virtually no one in the philosophical literature today.[5] Nevertheless, as should be clear, our analysis and criticism of torture under its various representative models will have a direct relevance to how we are to morally assess instances of torture used punitively. If torture is always immoral, it obviously follows that it is also immoral when used as a punishment for a particular crime.

The rough and ready characterization of the forms of torture should be sufficient to begin our exploration of the ethics of torture. The aim of making distinctions in kinds of torture, to reiterate an earlier point, is to attempt to better specify what torture actually *is*—or, more carefully put, it is to attempt to specify the family of various things torture is. Acknowledging the range of types of torture, as well as the explanatory models we use to analyze these kinds, enables us to grapple with torture in a much more sustained and systematic way. Having laid out the variety of types of torture, we will now turn our attention to those models of torture that are most often employed in the assessment of it.

MODELS OF TORTURE

It is our contention that the only way to grapple with the ethics of torture is to acknowledge that there are different *types* of torture, and that these types of torture can be examined under different models. This book consists of examining torture under four separate models. Under each of these models, we will demonstrate that torture—in all of its forms—is morally impermissible. By examining each of these models in some detail, we will prevent the common retreat of some defenders of torture from one model to another. Thus, when we emphasize the way that torture forces persons to use their very humanity against themselves (Chapter Three), or dismantles the individual agency of *even the torturer* (Chapter Four), or undermines the conditions of meaningful communication (Chapter Five), our opponent will not be able to retreat to the familiar utilitarian considerations of the ticking-bomb, as we will have already revealed that the ticking-bomb case cannot justify torture, and that our intuitions about torture in so-called "hard cases" are by no means as straightforward as many maintain (Chapter Two). By systematically examining the ethics of torture under its various models, we are able to present a comprehensive argument for the wrongness of torture. Our aim in this section is briefly to introduce the models under which torture can be understood. An initial approximation of the four models we will be examining in detail can be put as follows.

Economic Model

Understands torture as an exchange of pain and information, question and answer, costs and benefits. In this model, torture is a transaction between two agents, one wanting to acquire something from the other, and the other resisting such acquisition. Torture is thus an attempt to force the exchange to occur by making the stakes of refusing the exchange too high.

Phenomenological Model

Understands torture in terms of the experience of the tortured, paying close attention to how torture is structured experientially, and how the experience of torture alters one's experience of the workaday world one normally occupies.

Dramaturgical Model

Understands torture in terms of role performances in a figurative theater. Special attention is paid to the institutional features of a situation that enable individual actors to engage in torturous behavior, as well as the psychological mechanisms that enable this to occur (in-group/out-group thinking, dehumanization, de-identification, and so on).

Communicative Model

Understands torture in terms of the communicative relations between two subjects in discourse. Torture is understood through the lens of normal and abnormal discursive interactions between subjects.

By examining each of these models in detail, our aim is to demonstrate that torture cannot be morally or politically defended. Our strategy is to begin with the most common model of torture (the economic one) along with the most common arguments that attempt to justify torture (ticking-bomb arguments). Having established the illegitimacy of these arguments, as well as the limitations of this model, we will then proceed to analyze what it is that makes torture so reprehensible by examining its logic and structure. Before commencing this (substantial) task, however, it will be worth our time to briefly articulate some of the various positions taken on torture, if only to understand the terms in which the current debate is often carried out.

POSITIONS ON TORTURE

There are an astonishing number of diverse positions that one can take when it comes to torture. This is evident not just from the philosophical and jurisprudential literature on torture, but also from the history of the practice itself. There has never been a time when torture was not with us: it has always been there, albeit sometimes hidden in the shadows, and it seems unfortunately unlikely that it will ever disappear. There have been moments of intense hope—such as in the nineteenth century, when Victor Hugo was optimistic enough to proclaim that "Torture no longer exists." There was likewise such hope in the decades following World War II, when there was a renewed commitment to anti-torture treaties, such as the Geneva Accords, the UN Convention Against Torture, and the Universal Declaration of Human Rights. As we now know quite well, our optimism was misplaced. Even in those nations most vocally opposed to torture—in the democracies of the developed West—torture still takes place, apparently routinely.[6]

Although the primary aim of this book is to examine the ethics of torture in its current incarnations, our analysis will also apply to torture as it has manifested itself in other guises—in legal systems, court proceedings, and so on. To get a sense of the ubiquity of the problem, and the range of positions that have been taken both historically and in the contemporary debate, we offer the following range of positions, with brief historical and current examples.

Absolute Prohibition	Torture is never acceptable.	Nineteenth-century Humanists (Voltaire, Beccaria), in relation to court proceedings.[7] Jean-Paul Sartre, Ariel Dorfman, Henri Alleg, Jean Amery.
Limited Prohibition	Torture is permitted against certain persons and at certain times.	The Inquisition, Ancient courts (to ensure the testimony of slaves), and Medieval European Courts (for capital crimes).
Limited Legal Permissibility	Torture is permissible in certain (exceptional) cases.	Alan Dershowitz (when there is appropriate judicial oversight) and Stephen Kershnar (as punishment for certain crimes).
Limited Moral Permissibility	Torture, although *always* illegal, is permissible in certain cases.	Michael Walzer (in "Dirty Hands" cases), Israeli Supreme Court (Necessity Defense), Miriam Gur-Aye (on basis of Self-Defense),

		Oren Gross (as civil disobedience), Senator John McCain, along with *many* others (only in ticking-bomb case).
Absolute Permissibility	Torture is permissible in any context.	Nero, Marquis de Sade.

The range of positions presented here requires some (minimal) comment. In the current context, our primary interest will be on the two types of limited permissibility, both legal and moral, along with absolute prohibition (the view we will defend). The other views are important in recognizing the historical scope of torture. Absolute permissibility, it should be noted, has only been defended by a few (arguably insane) persons. Torture, in Nero's Rome, was something that literally anyone might face simply in virtue of Nero's rather indelicate sensibilities. The same is true of the Marquis de Sade, though Sade of course did not have the power of the state to back his sadistic ambitions.

Limited Prohibition, perhaps surprisingly, has been the *most common* position historically maintained. This has been largely due to the role of torture in the judicial and evidential proceedings of the West. Although the history of torture is a fascinating one, it is not our focus in the current context. Nevertheless, some mention of the previous role(s) of torture will provide a richer sense of just how pervasive this practice has been in the history of the West.

Torture in ancient Athens was fundamentally evidentiary. It was utilized as a means of insuring the truth of non-Greeks (the Greek term for torture, *basanos*, connotes testing the quality of metal by pressing it against a touchstone). The point was to utilize torture to establish the veracity of the testimony of a *third person* (*not* the defendant in a case). In Roman-canon law and the Middle Ages, this changes: torture remains evidentiary, but becomes a means of getting confessions from defendants. These confessions, however, were widely recognized as problematic. The legal system thus attempted to safeguard against false confessions. To this end, a mass of regulations surrounded the use of torture in the courts: torture had to be ordered by a judge, it could only be ordered when a "half-proof" of someone's guilt was available (one eye-witness, or large amounts of circumstantial evidence), no leading questioning was permitted (the accused needed to confess things that could be verified, such as the location of stolen goods, a body, or a murder weapon), and confessions obtained while under questioning were *inadmissible* in the courts. (The accused had to re-confess in the court, and there had to be a period of time—often 24 hours—between torture and the confession in court).

As Langbein has argued, this system developed out of the wreckage of the older trials by ordeal, where God was meant to decide on one's guilt or innocence. Ultimately, the system was abandoned, *not* because it was viewed as particularly inhumane, but because our standards for evidence *lessened* as we developed alternative punishments (such as prison sentences). We became willing to convict on circumstantial evidence, or with one eye-witness (the old system required either a confession or two eye-witnesses for conviction of a capital crime), largely because a conviction for a capital crime no longer meant death or dismemberment. As this change in the practice of evidence emerged across Europe, the need for torture in criminal proceedings diminished, and torture receded from the judicial stage.[8]

It was this disappearance which led to Hugo's conceit (recall his claim, in the mid-nineteenth century, that "torture no longer exists"). He was correct that it no longer existed in the court system—but it never disappeared from other venues. It is in these other venues that the current debates play out—and hence it is in these other venues that our own argumentative efforts will take place.

Recall that our primary concern in this book is to deal with arguments claiming that torture is permissible in limited contexts, either legally, morally, or both. These two positions (limited legal permissibility and limited moral permissibility) are *by far* the most prevalent in the current debate, with limited moral permissibility defended by far more authors—even those who have staunchly criticized torture policy—than limited legal permissibility. The difference in these two positions is fairly straightforward: advocates of limited legal permissibility typically advocate some form of judicial or executive oversight for cases where torture is deemed necessary to the interests of a state. Those who advocate moral permissibility (rather than legal permissibility) are against any kind of legal legitimation for torture, even if torture is (morally) justified in certain cases.

Alan Dershowitz has been the most vocal advocate of limited legal permissibility. In Dershowitz's view, torture is an inevitable feature of the modern world. Given torture's inevitability, we ought to create some type of oversight to ensure that torture is used only in the rarest of cases. This will allow us to monitor this practice closely rather than simply closing our eyes to its existence. By thus monitoring instances of torture, Dershowitz argues, we will actually *decrease* the amount of torture that is currently perpetrated in the world (for a critique of the argument, see Chapter Two).

A different argument for limited legal permissibility has been given by White House Legal Counsel under President George W. Bush (though, importantly, the term "torture" is never used). The argument attempts to establish that the President alone is permitted to order "torture" (or "torture lite," as it has often been called) despite whatever laws exist to the contrary. The argument runs as follows: laws (and treaties) are only legitimate insofar as they are consistent with the US Constitution. Any law in force must be interpreted as being consistent with this document. If no such interpretation is possible, the law has no validity. (This portion of the argument is uncontroversial). The US Constitution provides that the President of the United States is the Commander-in-Chief, and has the sole discretion to wage war and protect interests of national security in the way he or she sees fit. The Constitution also maintains that the President has the duty to execute the laws of the land and the duty to defend the Constitution. Thus, any law that limits the power of the President to conduct interrogations as he or she sees fit is unconstitutional, as it interferes with the ability of the President to protect the national interests of the United States as the Commander-in-Chief. As such, that law must either be understood as *not applying* to the President as Commander-in-Chief, or as being unconstitutional (and hence as invalid). Thus, if the President orders torture tactics to be used, he is legally permitted to do so.

This kind of legalistic argument, of course, does not yet touch the moral (im)permissibility of torture. Whether or not any leader *should* order the use of torturous interrogation techniques is left undecided. Presumably, one could fill in an argument for ordering torturous interrogation techniques as follows (and we presume that something very much like this argument is actually endorsed by many officials in the United States):

1. Torture is necessary to protect the interests of the citizens of the United States.
2. The interests of the citizens of the United States are to take moral precedence over the interests of other persons.
3. Therefore, torture is morally permissible.

Obviously, this argument leaves much to be desired. As we will see in the chapters to come, the first premise is by no means obvious. By our lights, it appears demonstrably false. The second premise is no less (morally) problematic. One's nationality—something that is normally the product of luck rather than effort—seems as morally arbitrary a reason for privilege as does one's race, sex, or sexual orientation.

The most prominent view in the literature on torture is, without qualification, the view that torture is morally permissible in limited circumstances. These circumstances are typically captured in what is called the "ticking-bomb" case: it is postulated that the only way to save several hundred (or thousand, or hundred-thousand) persons is to torture a prisoner you know to have planted a bomb in a densely populated urban area. Leaving aside the details of the thought-experiment (which will be considered in Chapter Two), most theorists seem to acquiesce to the view that it is morally permissible to torture in such a case. Some even insist that it is one's moral duty to torture. This is not to be confused with the view that torture should be *legal*. As always, questions of legality and morality ought to be carefully distinguished. Legalizing torture—even in rare cases—would have significant negative consequences (the argument goes). Thus, in cases where it is morally necessary to torture, the torturer must simply engage in an illegal action.

What is often debated in the jurisprudential literature is how best to handle such cases. Some have argued for what is called a "necessity defense" (such as the Israeli Supreme Court).[9]

The necessity defense maintains that one is not culpable for an illegal action because that action was *necessary* to maintaining one's life. Ticking-bomb scenarios, the argument goes, present such a case. A parallel defense, defended by Miriam Gur-Arye, is that torture in such cases can be defended on the grounds of self-defense.[10] This is superior to the necessity defense, Gur-Arye maintains, because necessity might justify the torture of innocent persons (whereas self-defense does not). Still others, such as Oren Gross, argue for the view that official civil disobedience is a better model for understanding torture in the ticking-bomb case.[11] Like Rosa Parks or Harriet Tubman, who broke laws in the name of justice, military personnel can claim acts of official disobedience when torture is morally necessary. Torture, when justified, should only be justified *after the fact.* Such "justification" could be in the form of a commuted sentence, a reduced sentence, a pardon, or the decision not to prosecute.

As is clear, these views of torture all rely on the presumed moral permissibility of torture. The arguments themselves are meaningless without this presupposition. It is this very presupposition that we will examine in this book. As we will show, the ticking-bomb argument that is so uniformly relied upon in this literature ought to be outright rejected. Moreover, as we will demonstrate, the wrongness of torture has been, in certain fundamental respects, *underestimated*—even by those few who happen to agree that there ought to be an absolute moral and legal prohibition on it.

In the following pages, we will systematically investigate torture as presented under four distinct models. We will demonstrate that torture is not to be accepted on *any* of the available models—even on the one that is most commonly used in the attempt to justify it (the economic model). Along the way, we will tackle the available arguments and positions that have been advanced in defense of torture as well as against it.

CHAPTER TWO

THE ECONOMIC MODEL OF TORTURE

TICKING-BOMB ARGUMENTS AND TORTURE WARRANTS

The most common conversations about torture tend to employ economic language: the give and take of question and answer, of pain and information, of possible costs and benefits. Indeed, the force of the most common argument *in favor* of limited permissibility (The Ticking-Bomb Argument) depends precisely on economic considerations: we are asked to imagine a scenario in which only torture will enable us to track down a bomb that is set to detonate in a densely populated urban area. The case is meant to draw on our more utilitarian intuitions—on our desire to save the many at the cost of merely one. If there is a seemingly compelling argument in favor of limited permissibility (which is, as the reader will recall, the most commonly defended view for the permissibility of torture), the ticking-bomb argument is it. Likewise, it is the strongest of "economic" arguments for torture, as it makes the benefits of the hypothetical torture quite high, and the costs (seemingly) low. It is thus incumbent on us to examine in detail this argument, and hence to explore whether or not a case can be made for the limited permissibility view.

THE TICKING-BOMB ARGUMENT, PART ONE: TORTURE AS MORALLY PERMISSIBLE

Imagine that you, an agent of the CIA, have just captured a well-known terrorist (let's say it's Osama Bin Laden). You have excellent information that there is an imminent attack planned on a major US city. This attack will involve the explosion of a nuclear device. You also know that this attack will be carried out within the next 5–10 hours, making evacuation impossible. As it happens, you are also an expert interrogator, skilled in the dark arts of torture. You are convinced that through applying various techniques of physical and psychological manipulation you will get a confession of the location of the nuclear bomb, and thereby save the lives of perhaps a million US citizens. The question is simple: do you move forward with the torture?

Consider what someone might say to those who answered "no." If you refuse to torture, even though this would result in saving a million lives, you are essentially claiming that your own moral rectitude is more important than the lives of those in danger. This is a kind of moral narcissism that constitutes a moral failing: we elevate ourselves above those who will suffer. Sometimes, one might argue, the moral thing to do is to sacrifice ourselves.

The defender of answering "yes" might also point out the following: most of us support imprisoning people against their will for long periods of time. Most persons also accept putting people to death when this is necessary for saving lives (such as in cases of self-defense, or in cases where a hostage taker is threatening the lives of a group of people). To accept the permissibility of killing in these cases while *denying* the permissibility of torture in a ticking-bomb case seems to be flat out contradictory. Death is, the defender might continue, worse than torture—so if killing is justified to save lives, so too must torture be. Saving a dozen hostages by killing the hostage-taker is significantly more morally problematic than torturing someone in order to save a million. This, then, is the force of the dilemma.

It is difficult to answer "no" to the question of torturing in this case, especially when one is pressed. Even Jeremy Bentham, a true activist for human well-being, thought that torture had to be permissible in certain cases.[1] This view has more recently been defended by the Harvard Law Professor Alan Dershowitz,[2] as well as a host of philosophers, legal theorists, and political scientists.[3] Even Senator John McCain, the most vocal of the advocates of the recent "torture ban," has acknowledged that scenarios such as the one described above constitute an exception to the ban he advocates.[4]

Responses to the argument, of course, differ tremendously. Some argue that this shows us that we should permit torture under certain judicial oversight. Others claim that this would legitimate torture, and hence that we should proceed on a case-by-case basis, allowing courts to decide *after the fact* if an instance of torture was justified.[5] Still others contend that torture should be *routinely* permitted, as it is no worse than many forms of punishment, and we routinely impose punishment on persons against their will in order to achieve a greater social good. (These authors typically use the above argument as a point of departure for the defense of their much broader acceptance of torture.)[6]

Cases like the one described above are routinely referred to as "ticking-bomb arguments." They are by far the most powerful case that can be presented to contest the view that, morally speaking, torture is always to be avoided. The structure of the argument is fairly straightforward: we posit an extreme case where intelligence is required to prevent a massive evil. We are then presented with a choice that seems to require choosing a *lesser* evil in order to avoid some disastrous consequences. Once we have conceded that in a case *like this* torture is permissible, all that is left to do (as George Bernard Shaw famously quipped) is haggle over the price. Given that we are willing to torture, we have to decide just *how* extreme the circumstances need to be to proceed. If we will torture for a million lives, will we do it for 100,000? 1,000? Four? In this way, the ticking-bomb argument is a wedge argument. It is the first step in defending a more general policy allowing torture in some instances, even if these instances are strictly supervised and quite exceptional.

It is easy for many to respond to such arguments with a slippery slope objection. If we allow torture in certain extreme cases, we will wind up allowing torture in less extreme cases. In order to avoid torture becoming pervasive, we must adopt a strict no tolerance policy for such practices. This line of argument, in many cases, is fallacious. As Bagaric and Clarke point out,

> laws that permit citizens to use self-help measures to inflict (even lethal) harm such as self-defense and necessity have not resulted in significant abuses. This is despite the fact that such laws are "gray" in application and the lawfulness of the conduct is generally evaluated after that fact. (46)[7]

Thus, it is insufficient simply to point out that a current policy might lead to one that is substantially worse. This "might" merely express a worry; it does not constitute an argument. As Bagaric and Clarke (correctly) argue, slippery slope arguments are objections only when they are based on *evidence* (like historical precedent). They cannot simply be invented.[8]

THREE INITIAL RESPONSES

The Dignity of Persons Objection

Perhaps the first response one might make to the above arguments is to meet utilitarian considerations with deontological ones. Rather than accepting that torture is like an economic transaction, where we trade one life for many others, one might emphasize a position typically associated with Kant: namely, the view that the respect of a given individual is inviolable, and is not the sort of thing that has a "price." Objects can be traded according to equivalences; human beings, however, cannot.

The problem with the ticking-bomb argument, every Kantian will insist, lies with the model of torture (and of ethical thinking and agency) that it presupposes. The numbers game ignores the individual dignity and autonomy of the agents subject to its analysis. Although there are powerful arguments against the economic model of ethical analysis, and hence of a defense of torture along economic lines, it is important in the current context to see if the argument above works *given* economic assumptions. If the argument can be shown to be lacking even when we reason within economic parameters (with the conception of torture as mere transaction), its rejection will prove all the more decisive. Thus, despite our own predilection to accept the Kantian conception of the person, to combat the ticking-bomb argument requires thinking about torture on the economic model that is the basis of the argument, at least if we prefer to avoid a standoff of moral intuitions.

Artificial Cases Objection

The other immediate response often offered by those confronted with the ticking-bomb argument typically involves pointing out how deeply artificial the case is. This objection is forcefully raised in Henry Shue's classic paper, "Torture"[9]:

> There is a saying in jurisprudence that hard cases make bad law, and there might well be one in philosophy that artificial cases make bad ethics . . . Notice how unlike the circumstances of an actual choice about torture the philosopher's

example is. The proposed victim of our torture is not someone we suspect of planting the device: he is the perpetrator. He is not some pitiful psychotic making one last play for attention: he *did* plant the device. The wiring is not backwards, the mechanism is not jammed: the device *will* destroy the city if not deactivated. (142)

As Shue makes clear, the ticking-bomb case is practically beyond belief. In addition to the above problems, we must also know how to torture the perpetrator, that torture will be effective, that it will not take more time than is available, and so on.

But the artificiality of the ticking-bomb case is in fact worse than any of this suggests: if we know that the bomb is wired correctly, and that *this* perpetrator is guilty of placing this bomb where it is, we must have acquired this knowledge in some way. How could we have the knowledge in question—a certainty that makes torture permissible—unless we *saw* the bomb being wired, and then *saw* this perpetrator place it? If we have seen these things, however, (and hence torture is permitted) there would be no *need* to torture.

Legitimation Objection

A final common objection to the ticking-bomb argument has received a good deal of publicity. This objection can be very quickly articulated. It comes in two basic forms, and stems from one particular insight: if we accept torture in some cases, we wind up making torture more legitimate than it currently is; if we concede that torture might be acceptable in some cases, we also decrease torture's deplorability in the minds of others, lending it a veil of legitimacy.

The strongest version of this view has been articulated by Žižek, who claims that *any discussion at all* (even this book) legitimates torture. On this view, then, we should simply remain silent, not dignifying torture with any analysis or conversation. A weaker version of this objection runs as follows: if we discuss torture, specifying, say, that we can employ psychological pressure on agents along with sleep deprivation and other tactics, but that we cannot inflict harsh physical pain on such agents, we (perhaps inadvertently) legitimate the use of *all and any* techniques that are perhaps just below the level of torture. If it is considered torture to keep someone awake for 20 hours, and hence is regarded as illegitimate, this position might lead persons to subject others to 19 hours and 59 minutes of sleep deprivation. The thought here is that establishing actual policies will show persons where the line is, so that they can approach it more frequently with impunity.[10]

REJOINDER TO THE CLASSIC RESPONSES

There is something right about each of the above objections— but they do not, in our view, silence our utilitarian intuitions quite forcefully enough. Indeed, it is difficult to know (at this point) whether or not these intuitions *can* be silenced. Moreover, it might well be thought that the above objections can be met. Various supporters of torture might reply as follows.

The Dignity of Human Beings

The most straightforward response to this particular objection runs as follows: a utilitarian perspective is perfectly compatible with a respect for the dignity of persons. This respect, however, must be absolutely egalitarian. No one person has any more dignity than any other: you are worth as much as I am in terms of our dignity, and the reciprocal of this holds as well. Nothing in the ticking-bomb argument, or our intuitions regarding it, contradicts this. Indeed, it follows from this view that we *must* torture. To not torture in a ticking-bomb case would involve elevating the dignity of the torturer above the millions who would be killed if torture were not undertaken. This is anti-egalitarian, and hence incompatible with a *true* respect for the dignity of *all* human beings.

Artificial Cases

We never have perfect knowledge. This is a reality of the human condition. To require perfect knowledge for action of *any* kind would result in chronic paralysis. Our standards of proof should certainly be high in *all* criminal cases but we cannot ask for absolute certainty as we will never get this. Moreover, the function of the argument is not about torturing under these exact conditions—it is about whether we *in fact* believe that there are no circumstances under which torture is acceptable.

The ticking-bomb argument is meant to be an intuition pump—something that allows us to assess whether or not we actually believe that torture is impermissible. Once we have established that we *do not* think this, we can argue about the conditions under which it is acceptable. Even if there is never a ticking-bomb case, exploring such a case allows us to better understand and express our intuitions regarding torture—and thus to have a point of departure for thinking through this issue. The ticking-bomb argument shows that appeals to the inhumanity of torture are insufficient to establish its impermissibility as such a response likely comes more from our conditioned responses to the word "torture" than to our actual moral intuitions about particular cases.

In response to worries about knowledge, a defender of torture might also claim that torture works along the same lines as evolution: even if a thousand different cases are tried that ultimately fail, if one successful case occurs, the endeavor has been worth its cost. Much as a thousand species must die for one successful species to emerge, so too must a thousand suspects be tortured to get one good lead. Thus, the fact that torturing often produces false leads is not really a very substantial objection when we play the numbers game. If one person in a thousand produces a piece of good information (information that could potentially save several thousand people), then a torture policy would be justified.

Problem of Legitimation

An obvious reply to the claim about legitimation would be to argue that this objection engages in fallacious slippery slope reasoning. Permitting torture in extreme cases does not amount to permitting it in all cases, nor need it lead to the view that humans do not have dignity. It *might* lead to this—and this is certainly a worry to be considered—but it seems very difficult to establish this causal consequence of permitting certain instances of torture with any high degree of probability.

A second response that might be made to this line of objection would simply be to bite the bullet: yes, one might concede, permitting instances of torture *would* legitimate it, but (a defender of this view might continue) this is what we *want* to happen. Our failure to engage in this kind of activity in the open has been a mistake.

We do not find all of these responses to the above objections particularly persuasive—but that does not mean these responses can simply be ignored. What the responses demonstrate is that the above objections are not sufficient to end the debate about the ticking-bomb argument. There are, however, several lines of objection which, in our view, *do* constitute a sufficient reason to cease utilizing these *forms* of argument when discussing the ethics of torture. It is to a consideration of these additional objections that we now turn.

WHY WE SHOULD REJECT THE TICKING-BOMB ARGUMENT

The Primary Objection to the Ticking-Bomb Argument

There is no problem in principle with artificial cases, but there are limits on what *kinds* of cases we can construct. For example, a case cannot violate what we know about the *nature* of the thing we are exploring. For example, if we were imagining cases involving, say, rabbits, we would have to stick with what we mean by "rabbit" in (grounded) ordinary language. Nothing particularly contentious is meant by this. If we were asked to imagine a rabbit that was a dog, for example, we would be right to insist that the request was nonsensical. Rabbits—and this seems to be part of the use of the term—are *not* dogs. Thus, imagining one animal that is a rabbit precludes imagining that *same* animal as a dog (at best, it could be some mixture of the two—a "dabbit" or "rog," if you like).

This is an incredibly important point when thinking about torture. When someone constructs a case of "torture," for example, in which no pain (mental or physical) is experienced, and in which said "torture" is willingly submitted to, or even enjoyed, by both parties, it just is not clear that we're talking about torture anymore. Now, this should not be exaggerated. *Perhaps* torture can be willingly submitted to.[11] The point here is that the burden of argument is on the person who constructs such cases to show us that she is still talking about what we know to be torture. (Likewise, a rabbit might be a dog—but before we infer anything based on such a case, we'll need some argument!)

This is the primary problem with ticking-bomb cases. It is *not* that they are unrealistic epistemologically (though they are), or practically (though again, they are), or even psychologically (here they are unrealistic as well). The problem, rather, is that what is being called "torture" strains credulity. In some versions of the argument, we are asked to imagine a practice that is done beneficently, that does not exceed necessary force, and that has no lasting effects on the torturer or the tortured. Examples of the ticking-bomb argument postulating these conditions simply exceed the bounds of what attributes can be reasonably predicated of torturer, tortured, and what brings the two together.

One might here concede this point, allowing for a more realistic portrait of the torture that would be inflicted in the ticking-bomb scenario: there will be too much pain, and it will have lasting effects on both parties to the torture. Moreover, the motives of the torturer, no matter how good they are initially, will ultimately deteriorate. For many, the "clear" intuition that we ought to torture will evaporate at this point—particularly once we acknowledge the reality that we will make mistakes about whom we are justified in torturing. But this is not a sufficient reason to reject the ticking-bomb argument. After all, there are many versions of the argument, and the above (unrealistic) conditions do not seem essential to the thought experiment.

What, then, is essential? Two things seem essential: (a) There is a finite amount of time before the bomb will detonate. The time in question makes alternative means of intelligence gathering unacceptable. Interrogation by torture is thus demanded given our time constraints. (b) A greater loss will occur as a result of a *failure* to engage in torture. We will argue that once we have fleshed out what is involved in information-gathering (or "interrogational") torture, we will be in a position to see that (b) is false in the ticking-bomb case. It is false because interrogational torture, to be effective, simply cannot be carried out in the amount of time postulated in the ticking-bomb argument. Once we give up (b), the ticking-bomb argument falls apart.

For the argument we intend to present against the ticking-bomb case to work, it is crucial to specify in some detail what the structure of this argument is. Importantly, we are not claiming that one cannot use highly unlikely scenarios to test our intuitions. We absolutely can and *should* do this. Hard cases are a good means of testing intuitions that must latter be captured by reflective theoretical ethics. But this is *not* to say that any kind of thought experiment will adequately test our intuitions. There *are* constraints on thought experiments, constraints that are *semantic* and *logical* rather than probabilistic.

To be clear: a thought experiment needs to be *logically possible* to be useful. If you ask me to imagine a triangle with four sides, for example, and I claim that I can do it—that does not demonstrate that there *are* four-sided triangles, or that it is possible for four-sided triangles to exist. Rather, it demonstrates that I do not adequately understand the semantic content of the term "triangle." Thought experiments cannot contain contradictions, nor can they involve (to put the same point differently) semantic impossibilities. Thus, if one asks "If you arrive at a place before you left it, would you be on time?" one is entitled to simply reject the case. It is not clear what is being asked. This is not tantamount to rejecting all possible thought experiments about time. It is an insistence that we do not steep ourselves in nonsense when we conduct such thought experiments.

So, is the ticking-bomb argument nonsense? It certainly does not initially appear to be. This might be the result of it *not* being nonsense (the usual view), or it might be the result of us simply leaving the semantic content of interrogational torture underdetermined (this is the view we will defend).

As we have seen (in Chapter One), the term "torture," by itself, is a term that cannot be characterized as having clear semantic borders: there are cases of domestic abuse that look quite a lot like torture;[12] the Middle Ages present us with torture as a judicial process; some cases seem to aim at information, while others aim at evidence, humiliation, or simply the expression of power. Nevertheless, as we suggested there, we can get much clearer about the semantic content of torture when we distinguish it into *types* and *models*. It is our contention that much can be said about each of these models, as well as about *types* of torture presented in particular models. Thus, we are currently examining *interrogational* torture on an economic model (the way it is usually presented, though of course we can look at this on dramaturgical, phenomenological, and communicative models as well—as we will in future chapters). This, indeed, is the conception of torture on which the ticking-bomb argument relies: the claim is that we need information (hence, the torture is interrogational), and that torture is acceptable given that it will save a greater number of lives (hence, the model is economic). (Recall that these two things are conditions (a) and (b) enumerated above.)

Despite the semantic promiscuity of terms like "torture," such sub-classifications permit us to gather relatively concrete semantic content. It may well be impossible to adequately define "torture." It is hardly impossible, though, to define "interrogational torture on an economic model." (We might start with something like the following: the intentional infliction of physical of psychological pain on a subject in order to acquire information from that subject. Pain is traded for potential information.) This specification permits us to understand in much greater detail what is involved in interrogational torture—how it works, what its limitations are, and so forth. (This is analogous, though *only* analogous, to the distinction of types of triangles enabling us to say much more about what is involved in each type.)

It is at this point that we can begin to flesh out the *nature* of interrogational torture. Importantly, we do not think that the nature of torture should be understood as resulting from *a priori* considerations. While we might well explore concepts that do not involve intentionality without reference to empirical facts about human beings, the same cannot be said about intentional concepts. In other words, the semantic content of terms like "want" and "desire" are determined (at least in part) by the putative nature of the creatures that can want and desire things. While we do not need to consider human beings to explore the semantic content of "triangle," we *do* need to consider human beings in talking about torture (indeed, it seems to be part of the semantic content of "triangle" that we do not need *in particular cases* to refer to the actions of persons to talk about the properties of triangles).[13] Torture is something that human beings *do*. As far as we know, it is something that *only* human beings do. There is thus no way of articulating the elements of torture without paying attention to it as a *practice*, and hence paying attention to human beings.

Thus, in considering what interrogational torture *is* and how it *works*, we will of necessity require some empirical content. This is an important point, as it demonstrates that semantic contradictions might be contradictions because of empirical facts (thus, there might well be necessary *a posteriori* truths about torture).

For example, if one postulated a thought experiment in which we had to begin by imagining that water was solid, and hence not wet, we could rightly point out that this violated the semantic content of "water." (We are not particularly interested in defending the view that semantic contradictions are fundamentally distinct from logical contradictions. With Wittgenstein, we regard the two as sharing a very blurry boundary. The line between the empirical and conceptual is often too fuzzy to make neat divisions.)

Before applying these remarks directly to the case of interrogational torture, there is an objection that must be met. One might very well contend that there are perfectly convincing thought experiments that involve semantic contradictions, and hence that the claims we have thus far been making cannot be completely correct. If a thought experiment can demonstrate x, despite relying on semantically nasty features, then surely this cannot be an objection to the ticking-bomb argument. An example of such a thought experiment is Judith Jarvis Thompson's famous people-seed example.

> Suppose it were like this: people-seeds drift about in the air like pollen, and if you open your windows, one may drift in and take root in your carpets or upholstery. You don't want children, so you fix up your windows with fine mesh screens, the very best you can buy. As can happen, however, and on very, very rare occasions does happen, one of the screens is defective; and a seed drifts in and takes root. (745)[14]

Using this example, one might argue as follows: This example, as wonderfully clever as it is, seems to rely on a semantic contradiction. While we certainly do not know everything about persons, we are as certain as we can be that they are not plants—that they do not grow from seeds. Thus, if this thought experiment works, the claim that thought experiments cannot rely on semantic contradictions must be false.

There are two lines of response here that are worth exploring. Determining exactly what response is appropriate in this particular case might well require a book, so we will limit ourselves to a few words. The point of enumerating these responses, then, is to make clear that this example is *not* a counter example.

We think this is likely as close as one might come to a counter example to the claim we have been defending (namely, that thought experiments *cannot* contain semantic contradictions), though, admittedly, other counter examples will need to be assessed on a case by cases basis.

(1) Although it is clear that persons are not plants, it is *not* clear whether or not embryos have the same status as persons. Thus, the appropriate analogue here is between the people seed and embryo (obviously). We cannot say that the embryo has the same status as a person, as this would beg the question. Indeed, the issue here is to test our intuitions about *whether or not* there is a semantic contradiction in the example. If we assume that there *is* such a contradiction, the thought experiment cannot do its job (namely, to *test* for contradiction). Analogously, if someone began the ticking-bomb scenario by saying "imagine an impermissible act of torture . . ." it could not test our intuition about whether or not torture was permissible in this case.

(2) Finally, the temptation to *accept* the thought experiment might well come from a disposition to accept what it shows (the permissibility of abortion). In fact, the plausibility of this case (in our view) stems largely from the *earlier* thought experiment (concerning the violinist) that effectively demonstrates the permissibility of abortion *without* committing semantic contradiction.[15] There is nothing contradictory in imagining being physically connected to another person such that the person has use of your organs. Given that, a few paragraphs earlier, this thought experiment went such a long way to establish the moral plausibility of removing life from one's body that depends on one, we are much more likely to accept that this thought experiment works on its own. If we imagine Thompson's argument *without* the initial violinist example, the force of the people-seed example is significantly weakened.

Any thought experiment that involves semantic contradictions should not be used as the basis of a position on a controversial topic. Its argumentative weight is significantly limited. This does *not* mean, though, that such thought experiments are entirely without value. As in the Thompson case, they might well re-enforce an already established position. Admittedly, though, this is of rhetorical, rather than argumentative, value.

Returning to the ticking-bomb argument, we are now in a position to explore the conception of torture implicit in (a) and (b) above, and explore whether or not this conception of torture runs afoul of the semantic content of interrogational torture (on an economic model). It is our view that it *does* run afoul, but to show this will require an examination of some of the features of effective interrogational torture. Recall that the claim made in the ticking-bomb argument is that interrogational torture will be effective in a relatively short amount of time. If it would not be effective, then this torture would not prevent a greater harm than it would cause (and hence (b) would be false).

It is relatively non-controversial to point out that the amount of torture required before any particular interrogatee divulges information cannot be predicted. Torture cannot be *timed* in advance (this agent will break in 2 hours). It is part of the nature of torture that there is simply no formula for what will work on particular persons at particular times. This is in fact part of the wisdom of interrogation manuals—and has been for a very long time (more on this in a moment). The significance of this, however, has been lost on the advocates of the ticking-bomb argument. It is part of the nature of *effective* interrogational torture, we will show, that one has potentially *limitless* time in which to conduct one's dark work.

The ability to draw out torture indefinitely is *crucial* to its potential effectiveness in virtually every case. If a detainee knows that they are free to give information after a certain period of time (say, 10 hours), this creates a strong incentive to maintain composure until it is no longer necessary. Virtually every interrogation manual in the modern era relies on the use of temporal confusion as a means of "regressing" a person to the point where they will talk. The 1963 *Kubark* Interrogation Manual remarks as follows:

> Some interrogatees can be regressed by persistent manipulation of time, by retarding and advancing clocks and serving meals at odd times . . . [this] is likely to drive him deeper and deeper into himself, until he is no longer able to control his responses in adult fashion. (77, quoted in McCoy, 93)

The CIA's *Human Resource Exploitation Manual,* compiled 30 years later as a revision of the *Kubark,* verifies that this tactic is tried and true:

> The "questioner" should be careful to manipulate the subject's environment to disrupt patterns, not to create them. Meals and sleep should be granted irregularly, in more than abundance or less than adequacy, on no discernible pattern. This is done to disorient the subject and destroy his capacity to resist. (L-3)

Indeed, psychological torture involves breaking down the identity of the person interrogated. Typical strategies involve sleep deprivation, time disorientation, and general strategies for multiplying confusion. (See section L-17 of the CIA *Human Resource Exploitation Manual,* which recommends things like rewarding non-cooperation and nonsensical questioning.) Breaking down the world of an agent (a phenomenon we will return to in later chapters), as well as the agent's own self-understanding, is crucial to making the agent a mere information-vomiting puppet. This is the very aim of torture—regression, which "is basically loss of autonomy."[16]

Of course, one might argue that the use of physical torture rather than psychological torture is what is required in ticking-bomb cases. Because psychological torture (the *preferred* kind, we hasten to remind our readers) cannot be adequately completed in a short span of time (our identity must be destroyed, and this *necessarily* takes time when approached psychologically), a ticking-bomb scenario requires the immediate application of brutal physical tactics.

Again, however, this type of argument seems to miss entirely the *nature* of torture—which of course includes the propensities of both torturer and tortured. As the authors of the CIA's *Human Resource Exploitation Manual* make clear, the use of physical torment from agents may well *prevent* the acquisition of information:

> The torture situation is an external conflict, a contest between the subject and his tormentor. The pain which is being inflicted upon him [the interrogatee] from outside himself may actually intensify his will to resist. On the other hand, pain which

he is inflicting on himself is more likely to sap his resistance. For example, if he is required to maintain rigid positions such as standing at attention or sitting in a stool *for long periods of time*, the immediate source of discomfort is not the "questioner" but the subject himself. His conflict is then an internal struggle. As long as he maintains this position, he is attributing to the "questioner" the ability to do something worse. But there is never a showdown where the "questioner" demonstrates this ability. *After a period of time*, the subject may exhaust his internal motivational strength. (my italics, L-12)

As we can see, the manual (which was used by the CIA to train torturers in South America and Asia, for example) points out that applying pain to a subject *from the outside* (such as hitting the agent) "may actually intensify his will to resist." Thus, in using pain, the recommendation is to use pain that results from the subject's *own body*. Of course, as the manual also points out, self-induced pain requires "long periods of time." Time is precisely what we lack in the ticking-bomb case.

What a defender of the ticking-bomb argument will likely state, in this instance, is that we must simply take off the proverbial gloves in an attempt to extract information more quickly. Rather than hitting and slapping, then, we remove fingernails with pliers, we smash toes with hammers, and we send electricity through the genitals. Once again, the CIA's *Human Resource Exploitation Manual* warns against this:

Intense pain is quite likely to produce false confessions, fabricated to avoid additional punishment. *This results in a time-consuming delay* while investigation is conducted and the admissions are proven untrue. During the respite, the subject can pull himself together and may even use the time to devise a more complex confession that takes still longer to disprove. (my italics, L-12)

The result here, I think, is clear: all interrogation takes time. If we want to acquire accurate information through torture, it simply cannot be done in a day using psychological means. The subject must be "regressed" to a state where there is no strong identity, where things no longer make sense. While one can increase levels of physical pain as a means to get information, this will likely result in subjects saying *anything at all*. Perhaps, eventually this will result in real information—but this, much like psychological torture, relies on time that we simply do not have in the ticking-bomb case. We must thus conclude that torture in the ticking-bomb case simply will not result in the saving of a million lives. Once we have adequately described the nature of torture—the tried and true techniques of government agencies the world over—we must concede that it is an ineffective means of acquiring information when the clock is running.

We should emphasize, again, that the point here is not that torture will *never* result in accurate information. It might very well (at least in a few cases) result in accurate information. But we are not at leisure to simply postulate that torture *will* work in the case we are considering. If effective torture, by its very nature, requires the judicious use of time, then postulating that torture can work in the ticking-bomb case (where time is limited) might well be like postulating that one can jump without moving. Any case that asks us to imagine such a case is intrinsically suspicious, and by no means should constitute the basis for a view that endorses torture either as policy or in particular cases. Indeed, if our exploration of *effective* interrogational torture has been adequate, we have shown that there is a semantic contradiction in the very idea of interrogational torture that can be effectively executed in a small amount of time, whether that time is 5 minutes or 5 hours.

Everything hangs on the immediacy of the impending bomb. It is this immediacy, however, that makes the thought experiment incoherent: there is no such thing as effective interrogational torture that lasts only 30 seconds. One does not need torture if a suspect is willing to talk, and if a suspect is not willing to talk, any method of coercion will require substantial time to be effective. This leads directly to a straightforward dilemma: if there's no time for alternative approaches to intelligence acquisition, then everything we know about interrogational torture tells us that this torture simply will not be effective. If there *is* time for other approaches to intelligence acquisition, then torture is unnecessary. Torture, in the ticking-bomb case, is thus either unnecessary or ineffective. This shows that (a) and (b) above are both to be rejected, and hence that every version of the ticking-bomb argument fails to justify this practice.

One Additional Objection

Some versions of the ticking-bomb argument, attempting to dodge the objection that allowing torture involves permitting sadism to run rampant, postulate that legitimate torture will always be done by someone motivated by virtue—by the need to save the lives of others. While this postulation is not intrinsic to the ticking-bomb argument, it is nevertheless worth some discussion, as it represents something endemic to discussions of torture: namely, a failure to appreciate its actual dynamics—to see it for what it is. As we have been contending, the only way we can see something for what it is *is to look*.

It is difficult to defend the claim that persons can be trained torturers (those who would need to engage in ticking-bomb torture for it to have a reasonable chance of success) without acknowledging that said persons will be affected by what they do—even if they are affected only *while they occupy the role of torturer*. As the voluminous research of social psychologists have shown, the mere occupation of a role is sufficient to produce *what is appropriate to that role* in persons of varying temperaments. This is precisely the result of Philip Zimbardo's famous Stanford Prison Experiment.

Now, it might be retorted that we are turning a conceptual thought experiment into an empirically laden thought experiment. We must concede this point, but with the caveat that thought experiments that are aimed at providing a foundation for *real policies* ought to have a basis in empirical reality, at the least. Minimally, they should not *ignore* the copious research that has been done. Moreover, as we argued earlier, thought experiments cannot ignore the nature of those things they aim to investigate.

FURTHER UTILITARIAN CONSIDERATIONS

But what do we do with someone who contends that time is not nearly so significant? Someone who contends that we might have someone for a *year* or more, and that person might possess information that will save lives if only we torture them? Once we admit this possibility, it seems we are in a position to expand the ticking-bomb argument even more. To demonstrate this, and also to look in more detail at a specific ticking-bomb argument, we will turn our attention now to one paradigmatic case of ticking-bomb reasoning in order to demonstrate that this reasoning results in unacceptable—and counter-intuitive—positions. In particular, any variation of the ticking-bomb argument that allows substantial latitude in regard to time (having a prisoner for several months, say), faces other particular objections: (1) there are alternative means of gathering information that do not involve torture, and (2) if we insist that torture is nevertheless acceptable (despite other means of evidence-gathering being at our disposal), we face a challenging consequence—namely, it looks as though it becomes acceptable to torture innocent persons, provided that their torture will facilitate learning more about how to more effectively torture the non-innocent.

To flesh out this *reductio*, we will turn to a recent attempt to justify a policy of torture based on instrumental (economic) reasoning. In their defense of a limited permissibility view of torture, Mirko Bagaric and Julie Clarke contend that "the way forward here is to obtain more pointed data regarding the circumstances in which torture has been effective and when it is failed" (60). Surprisingly, however, they go on to claim that "the study would have to be retrospective—no one would seriously contemplate actually torturing people for experimental purposes" (60).

Here we have the elements of a *reductio* that applies both to the specific view endorsed by Bagaric and Clarke, and to *any* view that claims torture is acceptable even when many lives are *not* immediately at risk.

As Bagaric and Clarke see it, certain conditions must be met for torture to occur. We must consider the following five things: "(1) the number of lives at risk; (2) the immediacy of the harm; (3) the availability of other means to acquire the information; (4) the level of wrongdoing of the agent; and (5) the likelihood that the agent actually does possess the relevant information."[17] There are *many* advocates of torture that do not think these five conditions need to be met in order to justify torture. However, even if we grant that these five conditions are necessary, we will show that this particular view results in absurdity. Thus, by dealing with the view put forward by Bagaric and Clarke (where there are substantial safeguards in place), we will also deal with those views that insist on fewer (if any) such safeguards.

Given the level of threat that those who are willing to use torture appear to perceive in the world today from "islamofascists" (to use the term Bagaric and Clarke use), the level of threat seems great indeed. Moreover, the lives at risk are great enough to warrant torture—even to make it a *duty,* at least according to Bagaric and Clarke (as well as others who are not so interested in safeguards against torturing those without knowledge of impending wrongdoing). Perhaps surprisingly, most people seem to meet conditions (1) and (3). The only potential conditions that are not met by *perhaps absolutely anyone* are thus (2), (4), and (5).

The conditions, however, *are met,* at least arguably so, by the majority of US citizens. First, proponents of these safeguards defend the safeguards as *things to consider.* They are not to be regarded as *decisive.* (If they were decisive, this view could be handled by the arguments given in the previous section.) The less immediate the threat, the more pause one ought to give to torturing particular persons—but each element is only *one* variable in the overall utilitarian calculation. However, in a state of crisis (such as the defenders of torture see in the world today), a threat looms everywhere (why else would torture be permissible?). Thus, given the current socio-political climate, condition (2) is met *for just about* anyone. What would prevent someone, then, from deciding to torture innocent persons?

Bagaric and Clarke do not defend the view that only actual terrorists are to be subjected to torture. In fact, they argue that anyone possessing information relevant to stopping future terrorist attacks can legitimately be subjected to torture—even if they are merely third parties. (Bagaric and Clarke, as well as others, point out that persons who are not themselves criminals are forced to testify, even at great risk to themselves, if they happen to have information relevant to criminal proceedings.) Thus, even innocent persons can be tortured on this view.

Notice that Bagaric and Clarke insist that that we must *know* a person has information before torture can commence. Other views are not so stringent. One might argue, along utilitarian lines, that only *some* evidence is required for the permissible use of torture. Regardless of what view one actually defends, this much is clear: one's innocence is irrelevant to whether or not one will be tortured. If one possesses information that will help agents prevent the loss of life, torture is permitted (at least when torture is considered on an economic model).

While this might give us some pause, the utilitarian argument tells us to nevertheless press on—for the good of the whole. In response to hard cases like the classic trolley problem or the lynching of the innocent person to put the mob at ease, Bagaric and Clarke contend that

> the correct approach is to accept this outcome . . . we are quite ready to accept that one should, or even must, sacrifice oneself or *others* for the good of the whole. The need to make such decisions is of course regrettable, but more regrettable still would be not making them and thereby increasing net human pain. (30–31)

It seems a very small step from here (if it is a step at all!) to notice that even if persons are *unaware* that they can disclose information that would help to save lives in the future, these persons are nevertheless obligated to provide this information. Being subjected to physical torment, it is easily seen, is one way in which a person can reveal information *about how the process of torture works*—about what is effective, what is not, and so on. This is sufficient to demonstrate that conditions (4) and (5) above have been met in even this case.

Now, this practice would of course be objectionable to someone (like the present authors) with strong Kantian inclinations. But it should not be objectionable *at all* for Bagaric and Clarke, or those who require fewer safeguards, to simply accept that sometimes innocent persons must die. The additional provisions of limited torture endorsed on this proposal would also be met. These include:

> (i) the motivation of the practice is compassion; (ii) it involves sacrificing the lower interest of one person to confer a greater benefit on another, (iii) it is almost certain that the subject has [or, "can provide"] the relevant information; and (iv) approval must be obtained from a state official. (45)

A good utilitarian judge might well allow such things on innocent persons, or perhaps just on felons, or the homeless, or others. Certainly, the motivation could be compassion. That is, if we accept that one can torture compassionately in order to save lives—a necessary condition for acceptable torture, on the Bagaric and Clarke view—then we can accept that one might torture *innocent people* compassionately for the same reason. As they bluntly state: "People who are simply aware of the threatened harm, that is, 'innocent people,' may in some circumstances also be subjected to torture" (36).

Finally, it is obvious that torture experimentation could provide useful data. So, unless we are prepared to say that torture is *never* acceptable (as we are—though this is not yet the time to defend this view), or that torture of the *innocent* is never acceptable (a view Bagaric and Clarke explicitly reject), then it seems we must accept the experimental torture of innocent persons (as a means to less painfully and more effectively torture future terrorists)—at least if we accept the argument provided by these philosophers. We, however, like Ivan and Alyosha in Dostoevsky's *The Brothers Karamozov,* are not willing to accept the torture of the innocent—even if it means creating paradise.

We thus have a contradiction at the very heart of this type of hard-line utilitarian defense (though certainly not of *every* kind of utilitarian defense). Bagaric and Clarke are committed to two incompatible views: (1) that experimental torture should not be seriously considered by anyone, and (2) that experimental torture is morally required, given the torture proposal they advocate.

There are other serious flaws with the arguments presented by Bagaric and Clarke—and in particular with the truncated, even somewhat glib, responses they give to objections that deserve more careful consideration. We must leave these worries for another occasion. In our view, though, the fact that the Bagaric/ Clarke proposal regarding torture commits us to (2) is sufficient to demonstrate its implausibility.

REVISITING THE THOUGHT EXPERIMENT

Before turning to an economic–political argument for torture, it will be useful for a moment to test our ticking-bomb intuitions one last time. This will be useful both as a means of more closely examining our initial reaction to the ticking-bomb argument, and as a means of extracting one of the useful lessons we can learn from the Bagaric/Clarke position. Recall the ticking-bomb case:

Case 1

Imagine that you, an agent of the CIA, have just captured a well-known terrorist (let's say it's Osama Bin Laden). You have excellent information that there is an imminent attack planned on a major US city. This attack will involve the explosion of a nuclear device. You also know that this attack will be carried out within the next 5–10 hours, making evacuation impossible. As it happens, you are also an expert interrogator, skilled in the dark arts of torture. You are convinced that through applying various techniques of physical and psychological manipulation you will get a confession of the location of the nuclear bomb, and thereby save the lives of perhaps a million US citizens. The question is simple: do you move forward with the torture?

Given our investigation of this argument thus far, now consider the following case—one that does not rely on inadequate time, and which derives from some of the considerations we have thus far been exploring.

Case 2

Imagine that you, an agent of the CIA, have been put in charge of a hospital somewhere in the United States. You are in a position to torture persons without punishment. You know that your torture will provide evidence for the proper way to torture future suspects, but you also know that it will take many decades, and dozens of persons, to perfect your methods. Indeed, most of your life will be spent torturing innocent persons in order to learn about the appropriate techniques to use. This will doubtless lead to less torture in the future, as your methods will perfect getting persons to talk in less time. The question is simple: do you move forward with the torture?

Our hunch is that our intuitions, in this case, will go the other way. Most people will say that we should not torture in this case. But notice that the logic of the two cases is essentially the same. Both rely on the view that by torturing some persons we will ultimately save many others. (We do not think that these intuitions will alter if we change the tortured to criminals of a variety of backgrounds.) Importantly, though, those who advocate torture without safeguards (or without sufficient safeguards) are more accurately represented in the thought experiment as it stands. What does this show? If we correct the ticking-bomb argument to allow for limitless time (if we change it to a slow-burn bomb, in other words), our intuitions no longer support the ticking-bomb case.

Of course, it might be objected that the counter example is unrealistic—or that it even contains a semantic contradiction. That it is unrealistic we do not deny. Whether or not there is a semantic contradiction seems an open question. Whether or not there is a semantic contradiction in the case, though, is irrelevant. Consider our alternatives: there's either a semantic contradiction or there is not. If there is not, we can change the ticking-bomb case to remove the semantic contradiction involving time (which was the source of our primary problem with the argument). If we do this, though, the example no longer produces results that support a torture policy (we don't think experimental torture is acceptable).

If there *is* a semantic contradiction in *Case 2*, it seems that we cannot accommodate the time change in the impending bomb. We have only added significant amounts of time to the original case. If we are willing to torture merely potential terrorists, or third parties who have knowledge of terrorist activity (as many defenders of torture are), then we are willing to torture the innocent. This is no different from torturing persons in order to obtain information about *how* to torture (as we argued above).

So, this entails that there is no way to save the ticking-bomb argument against the objections raised above concerning its use of time. If this is so, then any semantic contradiction in *Case 2* actually shows that the ticking-bomb argument is an inadequate one—and one that cannot be saved by tinkering with time. Thus, if *Case 2* fails, we likewise have no support for any policy which relies on a ticking-bomb argument.

VERSIONS OF THE TICKING-BOMB ARGUMENT, PART TWO: IMMORAL BUT POLITICALLY NECESSARY

Even if we acknowledge that torture is fundamentally impermissible, we might still claim that, as a matter of policy, torture is in some instances required. As paradoxical as this might sound, it is precisely this position which is defended by Michael Walzer in his seminal essay "Political Action: The Problem of Dirty Hands." It is likewise defended by Alan Dershowitz, who claims that despite the moral abhorrence of torture *in all cases*, as a matter of protecting the citizens of a nation, those who elect to serve that nation have a duty to do things such as torture. Thus, even if persons accept that torture is morally unacceptable, it might nevertheless be necessary for politicians (or other agents of the state) to engage in it. This is the view that we must now consider.

The Argument for Torture Warrants

Unlike many versions of the ticking-bomb argument (where the use of torture is hypothetically postulated as the only way to save innocent lives), Dershowitz's defense of torture is aimed at *reducing,* rather than morally justifying, the use of torture. As Dershowitz has repeatedly claimed, in print and in interviews, torture is morally repugnant. This (intuitive) view, however, is insufficient (on Dershowitz's view, as on Michael Walzer's) to decide whether or not torture might be politically justified in particular cases. Dershowitz claims that, given the inevitability of torture, as a democracy we simply *must* provide some judicial oversight of this practice. Such oversight (in the form of "torture warrants"), Dershowitz claims, will *limit* the amount of torture currently practiced by agents of the US government. As Dershowitz plainly claims, the "goal [of the advocacy of torture warrants] was, and remains, to reduce the use of torture to the smallest amount and degree possible, while creating public accountability for its rare use" (TR, 259).[18]

Dershowitz's defense of torture, of course, is predicated on the notion that torture is a fact of political reality—and one we have no chance of eliminating. This view leads him to pose the torture question as a sharp either/or:

> if torture is being or will be practiced, is it worse to close our eyes to it and tolerate its use by low-level law enforcement officials without accountability, or instead to bring it to the surface by requiring that a warrant of some kind be required as a precondition to the infliction of any type of torture under any circumstances? (TR, 257)

The dichotomy is a false one.[19] If these were our only options (use of torture by low-level officers with no accountability or use of a warrant), there would not be much of a choice. But the issue is *not* simply a decision between accountability and its absence.

The Dershowitz proposal has been subjected to a number of criticisms, most of which are quite perceptive. These criticisms usually point out that torture warrants would (1) lead to the increase of torture, (2) face immense practical obstacles, (3) degrade the judiciary, and (4) degrade "the core values on which the democratic state rests" (365).[20] I will not rehearse arguments adequately—and often more than adequately—made elsewhere.[21]

Our aim in this chapter is to demonstrate that Dershowitz's either/or, resting as it does on a claim about the efficacy of torture warrants, faces several (perhaps lethal) lines of objections. After demonstrating that using torture warrants (on the basis of their supposed ability to reduce instances of torture) is unwarranted, we will turn our attention (albeit briefly) to what we regard as a rather strange tension in Dershowitz's work between the need for debate in a healthy democracy, on the one hand, and his rather undemocratic argument that torture warrants are required if torture is inevitable.

The Diminished Harm Argument

Dershowitz claims that torture warrants might actually decrease the number of torture cases that occur. As he says, "I cannot see how [a warrant requirement] could possibly increase [torture], since a warrant requirement simply imposes an additional level of prior review" (TR, 270). In this section, we intend to demonstrate three ways that warrants might have no efficacy in diminishing the harm inflicted by torture by reducing its occurrence. We will then suggest why torture warrants might actually *increase* the amount of torture currently practiced in the world.

A Logical Argument against Efficacy

The creation of a process of judicial review along Dershowitzian lines would legalize certain instances of torture (viz., those that were conducted after a warrant for said torture was acquired). The problem in our current situation, however, is that despite torture's *illegality* people are still engaging in it. This demonstrates a disregard for the commitment to law, as well as a disregard for the seriousness of torture. Establishing a level of judiciary review could not possibly fix *this* problem—and it is this (a failure to respect the law in regard to torture) that is arguably the source of our current predicament. Making some instances of torture legal will not get people to respect the law regarding torture any more than an outright legalization of *all* torture would. Thus, it seems strange to claim that judiciary review would decrease the occurrence of torture. Asking people to acquire a torture warrant to limit the occurrences of torture may well have no effect at all, given that telling people that *all torture is morally abhorrent and illegal* does not prevent torture. Establishing a review process will not get those who currently do not respect the rule of law to miraculously *begin* respecting the law. It thus seems, in our view, that torture warrants will have little effect—with the exception that some torture might occur with even more impunity.

In defense of the view that torture warrants would facilitate the decrease in instances of torture, Dershowitz has presented the following examples.

a. Alleged wiretaps of Martin Luther King, Jr. "This was in the days when the attorney general could authorize a national security wiretap without a warrant. Today no judge would issue a warrant in a case as flimsy as that one" (TR, 271).
b. The detention of Zaccarias Moussaui "after trying to learn how to fly an airplane, without wanting to know much about landing it" (TR, 271). In this case, no warrant was sought, because it was believed that one would not have been granted.

If the torture case is like these, Dershowitz contends, requiring warrants will prevent instances of torture, much as requiring warrants now for wiretaps (arguably) has the effect of limiting the number of wiretaps used.

Let us ignore the questionable view that fewer wiretaps are currently used. Even if what Dershowitz says about these cases is accurate, these cases cannot be said to be analogous to the case of torture. When wiretaps did not require a warrant, there was not a disincentive to use them (it was not illegal to use them). In the case of torture, however, there *is* a current disincentive (viz., torture is illegal, against the sworn policy of the United States, a signatory of the International Convention against Torture). Changing the law, in the case of warrants, actually *creates* a disincentive where none existed (using wiretaps becomes illegal). Torture warrants, however, would *not* create a disincentive (torture is *already* illegal). The most it would do would be to encourage people to acquire warrants when they had a reasonable chance of doing so. If they failed to get a warrant, or thought that they would not get said warrant, there would be no *additional* disincentive for refraining from torture. With or without a warrant, torture in such a case is illegal. This, we think, is sufficient to show that Dershowitz cannot rely on these particular examples to demonstrate that torture warrants would have an impact on the number of occurrences of torture in any country that instituted a policy requiring such warrants.[22]

Dershowitz offers the following response to this line of objection:

> There are of course no guarantees that individual officers would not engage in abuses on their own, even with a warrant requirement. But the current excuse being offered—we had to do what we did to get information—would no longer be available, since there would be an authorized method of securing information in extraordinary cases by use of extraordinary means. (TR, 276)

To call this a response is actually rather generous. Dershowitz is indeed acknowledging the issue—but he offers no additional argument against the objection just raised. Rather, he seems here to simply re-assert his view. Moreover, it is unclear in what sense it is true that the excuse of "seeking information" will be unavailable. Torturers could simply claim that the judiciary review overlooked their case, or that there was not adequate time to seek judiciary approval. It is in the nature of excuses that they are infinitely adaptable. No warrant process will make this less so.

An Historical Argument against Efficacy
In *Why Terrorism Works*, Dershowitz claims that evidence for his view about the efficacy regarding torture warrants can be culled from the pages of history. The practice of European

courts in the sixteenth century, where torture warrants were commonly issued in order to acquire a confession from a suspect, does indeed present an example of the use of something akin to torture warrants—but this example hardly demonstrates what Dershowitz thinks it does.

Dershowitz thinks that this historical precedent constitutes evidence for his case that torture warrants can be an effective means of limiting the occurrences of torture, and that it can be appropriately used as a means to save lives.

> We find it difficult to imagine a benign use of nonlethal torture to save lives . . . but there was a time in the history of Anglo-Saxon law when torture was used to save life, rather than to take it, and when the limited administration of nonlethal torture was supervised by judges, including some that are well remembered in history. (WTW, 156)

Dershowitz, it should be noted, is simply mistaken here. Torture was *never* a part of English judicial proceedings. Judges *could not* issue torture warrants. The Privy Council could issue such warrants, for a brief period, but this never became part of standard judicial procedure. As Langbein unequivocally states, "The system of judicial torture was never known in England" (99, "The Legal History of England," op. cit.). As Langbein explains, "because the English never lodged the power to investigate under torture with ordinary law enforcement officers or courts, this century of experiment with torture [1540–1640] left hardly a trace in the Anglo-American criminal procedure" (ibid., 100). Moreover, the extra-legality of torture during this period was attested to by the best legal minds of the day. Thus, when Dershowitz writes that "the English system of torture was more visible and thus more subject to public accountability," he is simply mistaken (158).

But Dershowitz might have appealed to the situation in continental Europe to provide historical examples of the use of torture warrants. In European courts in this period, a series of restrictions developed around the use of torture to obtain evidence. To establish the guilt of those being prosecuted for "blood sanctions," a prosecutor required either two eye-witnesses to the crime or a confession on the part of the suspected criminal. These high standards of proof also explain the substantial restrictions surrounding the use of torture: one could torture *only* when there was either one eye-witness or substantial circumstantial evidence establishing the probable guilt of the person to be tortured—and then only if the courts agreed that the evidence warranted proceeding with the torture (in effect, issuing a torture warrant). Moreover, questioning under duress could not be leading. The suspect needed to provide information that could be corroborated by the courts (such as the location of a murder victim, or a weapon, or of stolen goods). The confessions procured through torture were, then as now, inadmissible in courts. Thus, the confession had to be repeated in the court when no torture was taking place.[23]

But does this historical precedent actually show what Dershowitz claims that it does? As Dershowitz admits,

it is always difficult to extrapolate from history, but it seems logical that a formal, visible, accountable, and centralized system is somewhat easier to control than an ad hoc, off the books, under-the-radar-screen nonsystem. I believe, though I certainly cannot prove, that a formal requirement of a judicial warrant as a pre-requisite to nonlethal torture would decrease the amount of physical violence directed against suspects. (WTW, 158)

As Steinhoff has (correctly) remarked, Dershowitz "should offer something more than his personal 'belief' " (op. cit., 347). As we have thus far seen, there are substantial *logical* problems with the view that warrants are likely to decrease the frequency of torture. As we argued above, for those who act *regardless* of the law, warrants will likely make no difference whatsoever to their conduct. A failure to get a warrant will not necessarily translate into refraining from torture. Nevertheless, it might well be the case that a judicial procedure would limit the number of others who might engage in the practice. (Though, again, the opposite argument seems just as plausible: those who refused to torture based on its illegality might now *pursue* torture as a means of interrogation in cases where they would not have done so before.) Does the European case give us reason to think one thing rather than another?

Dershowitz thinks that Langbein's work constitutes evidence for his view. Langbein, however, does not agree. As Langbein points out,

> the European law of torture was suffused with the spirit of safeguard, yet it was never able to correct for the fundamental unreliability of coerced evidence . . . I see little reason to think that modern circumstances would make investigation under torture more reliable . . . History's most important lesson is that it has not been possible to make coercion compatible with truth. (101)

Obviously, Langbein could be wrong about what history shows, and Dershowitz could be right. It will not do to simply appeal to authority in this case as an absolute arbiter in the dispute about what the historical record shows. However, it does make considerable sense to pay attention to those who have a strong familiarity with the historical record, all the while acknowledging their fallibility. Given that Dershowitz acknowledges the authority of Langbein's analysis of the historical record of torture—and indeed even relies on this analysis—we have reason to seriously consider Langbein's appraisal of this record when considering Dershowitz's proposal. No one would dispute, we think, which of these two men has more familiarity with the historical documents. Although this certainly *does not* demonstrate that Dershowitz's interpretation of the judicial system of Europe in this period is mistaken, it does demonstrate that there is substantial reason to insist that Dershowitz provide much more argument to establish his case. In short, the claim that the historical record shows us that torture warrants can be effective and that, moreover, these warrants will result in a decrease in the instances of torture, simply has not been adequately justified.

An Empirical Argument against Efficacy

There is a rather surprising set of empirical data, collected and analyzed by Oona A. Hathaway in "The Promise and Limits of the International Law of Torture,"[24] that is of relevance to the current issue. As we will argue, Hathaway's analysis provides some evidence for the view that torture warrants will *not* decrease instances of the use of torture (though the evidence certainly does not constitute proof).

Instituting judicial review of torture (i.e. having torture warrants) would essentially make torture a legal activity insofar as a warrant was issued. If torture were so legalized in the United States, this would constitute, essentially, a breach of the UN Convention against Torture. We here assume that such a breach would constitute a renunciation of this particular legal document by the United States. There is a tricky legal issue here, as, according to the US Senate, "cruel, inhuman or degrading treatment or punishment" is interpreted to cover only those things "prohibited by the Fifth, Eighth, and/or Fourteenth Amendments."[25] As John Parry sums up, "the Senate declared that the convention bans conduct that is already unconstitutional" (150).[26] Thus, if "torture" were legalized (and survived any potential threats to its constitutionality), it would not be "torture" as defined in the version of the UN Convention against Torture that the United States ratified. We will not spend any time considering this rather sophistic argument. Let us simply assume that torture warrants are warrants for actual torture.

Hathaway has analyzed the practices of over 160 nations over a 40-year period in an attempt to understand the effect of the UN Convention against Torture on actual torture practices.[27] Hathaway has found what can only be described as surprising results.

To wit: "nondemocratic nations that reportedly use torture frequently are *more* likely to join the Convention than nondemocratic nations that reportedly use torture infrequently" (202); moreover,

> as democracies' torture ratings grow worse, they are increasingly less likely to make legal commitments that prohibit them from engaging in torture . . . the opposite is true of dictatorships: those with worse reported torture practices are more likely to join the Torture Convention than those with better reported practices. (203)

The explanation for this asymmetry, on Hathaway's (quite plausible) account, has to do with the presence of effective domestic institutions. Dictatorships are quick to sign the Convention due to the high benefit to cost ratio. Because there are no *internal* mechanisms for the enforcement of international law in dictatorships, and because occurrences of torture are difficult to detect by other states, the commitment of a nondemocratic state to the Convention has virtually no downside. "States join treaties like the Convention against Torture in no small part to make themselves look good . . . they may hope to attract more foreign investment, aid donations, international trade, and other tangible benefits" (207).

In democracies, on the other hand, there *are* domestic institutions by which international agreements can be enforced. As Hathaway argues, "much of international law is . . . obeyed primarily because domestic institutions create mechanisms for ensuring that a state abides by its international legal commitments, whether or not particular governmental actors wish it to do so" (206). In states that lack the ability to create such mechanisms, worries about enforcement of international law by domestic means are substantially diminished, if they occur at all.

Now, it would certainly be too hasty to conclude from this data that all democracies *not* taking part in this treaty are engaged in more torture than those that are. The data presents correlation, after all, not cause. For the same reason, we cannot infer that a single state, were it to abandon its commitment to the Convention, would thereby *increase* the amount of torture in which it engaged. The (plausible) cause postulated in Hathaway's analysis (in the case of democratic states) might not work the same way in reverse. That is, even if the ability of domestic institutions to enforce international law can explain why certain democracies are less likely to sign the Convention (namely, because signing the Convention would require a potentially high cost—namely abandoning practices of torture), it doesn't follow from this that a state that abandoned its commitment to the Convention will thereby, automatically, increase its torturous practices.

To put this point bluntly, the data in Hathaway's work does not constitute a refutation of Dershowitz's efficacy claim regarding torture warrants (nor, of course, was it meant to). But while we do not have a refutation of Dershowitz's claim, we do have, at an absolute minimum, data that offers an additional reason against his hunch that torture warrants will diminish the instances of torture in the United States. Given what we know about democracies who are not signatories of the Convention, claims that those who are no longer claiming to follow the Convention will *decrease* torture deserve additional skepticism and scrutiny. It is this, we think, that Dershowitz owes us before we take seriously his proposal for the use of torture warrants.

The United States as Role Model for International Law

There is a final objection that we want (briefly) to mention. The objection, as the one before, is not decisive. Rather, it provides an additional reason to pause when considering the Dershowitz "torture warrant" proposal. Dershowitz claims that the United States sets precedent in international law when it makes particular legal decisions at home. If this is correct, then establishing a torture warrant policy might actually increase the total amount of torture in the world, as those nations who would have been less likely to engage in torture might well follow the lead of the United States.

We mention this objection only because it demonstrates, in our view, some of the fuzzy thinking surrounding Dershowitz's proposal. Although Dershowitz might well claim that he is only concerned with US torture, such an assertion seems like a disastrously short-sighted one. When we are talking about decreasing torture, we must consider this in terms of the international scene. If Dershowitz is moved by the ticking-bomb argument, he should also be moved by an analogous one: if the United States tortures, it will lead other nations to torture. Thus, unless we take an absolutist stance *against* torture (something that Dershowitz regards as bad, much like torturing) there will be disastrous consequences (a greater evil that must be avoided, much like the detonation of a ticking bomb). The logic of the ticking-bomb argument here works against one of its advocates.

The No-Hypocritical-Democracy Argument

Dershowitz thinks that torture, if it is to be used at all, *must* be used under judiciary (or perhaps executive) rule. The majority of US citizens (as well as citizens of many other countries) are sometimes said to think that torture is acceptable in ticking-bomb cases.[28] If this is indeed the will of the people, Dershowitz contends, then we should subject this policy to the appropriate oversight. A "don't ask, don't tell" policy on torture, in Dershowitz's reasoning, is simply unacceptable.

Dershowitz's case for torture warrants makes heavy use of the worry that *not* having some sort of judicial review will lead to a nation of hypocrisy. This, it might be objected, misplaces our moral priorities. While it is certainly morally lamentable to engage in hypocrisy, this is hardly comparable to engaging in torture! To suggest, as Dershowitz does, that our hypocrisy is a reason for an open torture policy is, one objection runs, a severe overestimation of the importance of practicing what one preaches.

A quick example will bring the force of this objection out. Imagine an avid killer who kills only in secret. This killer routinely speaks out against killing. We might imagine he even works for a company that attempts to thwart human rights abuses. Now, certainly this hypocrisy is lamentable. What this hypocrisy is *not,* however, is a reason for our killer to begin to claim that his killing is acceptable when he does it under the right conditions. Even if it *is* right, the attempt to avoid hypocrisy is no reason to *defend its rightness.* Indeed, the *only* reason to defend a true claim is *that it is true.* (This same example can be given with a hypocritical smoker, smoking is secret, and telling others not to. His hypocrisy is not a reason to endorse smoking.)

But perhaps this is unfair to Dershowitz. Perhaps there is a subtler view that leads to the condemnation of hypocrisy (at least in a democracy) with such vehemence. In responding to worries about the possible legitimation of torture through the introduction of legal warrants,[29] Dershowitz remarks that "off-the-book actions below the radar screen" are

> antithetical to the theory and practice of democracy. Citizens cannot approve or disapprove of governmental actions of which they are unaware . . . In a democracy governed by the law, we should never want our soldiers to take any action that we deem wrong or illegal. A good test of whether an action should or should not be done is whether we are prepared to have it disclosed—perhaps not immediately, but certainly after some time has passed. (WTW, 152)

So, what seems to lurk behind Dershowitz's hatred of hypocrisy is actually a rather compelling view: at the heart of democratic governance (at its best) is deliberative practice. To ignore secretive practices pretending they do not exist, in Dershowitz's view, would be a disastrous development for our nation—one that would tear at the very essence of what's worthwhile in democratic governance.

This claim about democracy is absolutely compelling. The existence of practices that are not subject to scrutiny and critical evaluation *is* antithetical to democracy. What we dispute is that this point *warrants engaging in torture*. This is simply non-sequitur. What it warrants is a *moratorium* on torture until we've had an adequate debate. Dershowitz is right to say that "if we tolerate torture, but keep it off the books and below the radar screen, we compromise principles of democratic accountability" (WTW 153), but he is mistaken to maintain that this constitutes support for the torture warrant policy. To institute a torture warrant policy so that we have judicial oversight of a once-secret practice is itself *antithetical to democracy*, at least if such a policy is not the result of clear thinking and argument among the citizens within that democracy. If there were not a clear majority in favor of such practices, then we should tread much more carefully.

Of course Dershowitz claims, based largely on anecdotal evidence, that the majority of US citizens are in favor of using torture in *some* cases (based on the responses of his law students to questions asked in class). There is some data to consider. A *Newsweek* poll finds the following:

> Most Americans and a majority of people in Britain, France and South Korea say torturing terrorism suspects is justified at least in rare instances, according to AP-Ipsos polling . . . The United States has drawn criticism from human rights groups and many governments, especially in Europe, for its treatment of terror suspects. President Bush and other top officials have said the U.S. does not torture, but some suspects in American custody have alleged they were victims of severe mistreatment . . . The polling, in the United States and eight of its closest allies, found that in Canada, Mexico and Germany people are divided on whether torture is ever justified. Most people opposed torture under any circumstances in Spain and Italy . . . In America, 61 percent of those surveyed agreed torture is justified at least on rare occasions. Almost nine in

10 in South Korea and just over half in France and Britain felt that way ... The polls of about 1,000 adults in each of the nine countries were conducted between Nov. 15 and Nov. 28 [of 2006]. Each poll had a margin of sampling error of plus or minus 3 percentage points.[30]

Now, 61 percent is a majority. But notice, the commitment to a practice of open debate in democracies *does not* amount to majoritarian rule. If Dershowitz wants the policy debated, he cannot rely on this (rather narrow) margin to justify implementing a policy of torture warrants. There is reason to suspect that our data on the purported acceptability of torture is colored, not by rational deliberation and scrutiny, but by the post-9/11 *zeitgeist*. Indeed, much of the dialogue about torture has not had the status of actual deliberation, focusing instead on prejudicial, irrational attitudes, and on scenarios that have little concrete relevance to a debate concerning torture warrants. Moreover, the polling data is not consistent. Consider data collected from a (much larger) poll, where participants were asked what position was closest to their own (all results are given in percentages; the positions stated in the poll are listed at the top of the table).[31]

As this makes clear, it is by no means evident that the majority of US Citizens *do* support the use of torture in particular cases. Whereas the *Newsweek* poll has the number at 61 percent, the BBC poll has the number at 36 percent. It is difficult to know which poll more accurately represents the actual beliefs of US citizens. Nevertheless, as we have hopefully shown, even *if there is* a clear majority of supporters at this time, this is not sufficient to implement the Dershowitzian proposal. As Dershowitz himself acknowledges, an actual debate concerning the very existence of torture is what is required.

Interestingly, Dershowitz's call for debate stands in remarkable tension with his claim that the inevitability of torture constitutes a reason for implementing his policy recommendation (the claim, the reader will recall, with which we began). It seems Dershowitz wants a debate about the *frequency* of torture rather than about its appropriateness (at least when he focuses on his inevitability argument). If what matters is debate, then the inevitability of torture is *irrelevant* in a democracy. What matters is openness about what is happening on the ground, and the

BBC Global Torture Poll, 2006

Country	Terrorists pose such an extreme threat that governments should now be allowed to use some degree of torture if it may gain information that saves innocent lives	Clear rules against torture should be maintained because any use of torture is immoral and will weaken international human rights standards against torture	Neither/Don't Know
Australia	22	75	3
Brazil	32	61	8
Canada	22	74	4
Chile	22	62	16
China	37	49	13
Egypt	25	65	9
France	19	75	6
Germany	21	71	7
India	32	23	4
Indonesia	40	51	45
Iraq	42	55	8
Israel	43	48	1
Italy	14	81	9
Kenya	38	53	6
Mexico	24	50	9
Nigeria	39	49	27
Philippines	40	56	12
Poland	27	62	5
South Korea	31	66	12
Russia	37	43	19
Spain	16	65	3
Turkey	24	62	19
Ukraine	29	54	14
UK	24	72	18
USA	36	58	7
Average:	29	59	12

willingness to subject it, as well as the policy around it, to critical scrutiny. If the inevitability argument works, though, our deliberations about *allowing* torture are irrelevant, as it will happen regardless of our deliberation (and hence we should have a policy of warrants, claims Dershowitz).

We see no easy way to resolve this tension. Dershowitz cannot defend both arguments without inconsistency. If he opts to defend the view (which we accept) that we must have an open debate about our policies, then he has *not* established that torture warrants are warranted on the basis of a desire for accountability. If, on the other hand, Dershowitz thinks that the inevitability of torture warrants the use of torture warrants, it follows that the debate about whether to allow torture is a non-starter. But Dershowitz cannot, so far as we can see, have it both ways.

In this section we have argued that Alan Dershowitz's torture warrant proposal, at least as it stands, ought to be abandoned. We have argued that his view that judicial review will *decrease* the instances of torture can be challenged on four grounds. We have further suggested that Dershowitz's arguments (based on accountability and inevitability) cannot consistently be presented, and that, moreover, neither argument actually warrants a policy of torture warrants.

CONCLUDING THOUGHTS

As we hopefully have shown, the most well-known arguments in support of torture (institutionally supported or not) face serious difficulties. The difficulties we have concentrated on thus far, we must concede, are not even the strongest available. Those will be presented in the following three chapters. Nevertheless, even when we take the economic model on its own terms, we see that it leaves much room for doubt with regard to the moral and political acceptability of torture. In fact, we think we have shown that the best arguments available for torture on the economic model simply do not work. The more concrete the argument, the more basic its flaws.

But it is not enough to show that the economic arguments face serious difficulties. We must also show that the difficulties such arguments face lead to the unsustainability of the positions advocated. It is to this task that we turn in the following chapters. These additional arguments will explore alternative models of torture—models, as we pointed out in Chapter One, which are not meant to be regarded as mutually exclusive. It is our contention that these additional arguments will seal the coffin on the ticking-bomb scenario, as well as on the intuitions that it seems to excite.

CHAPTER THREE

THE PHENOMENOLOGICAL
MODEL OF TORTURE

DIGNITY AND THE DESTRUCTION
OF AGENCY

Perhaps the most perplexing aspect of the torture literature that aims to *defend* limited uses of interrogational torture is its seeming ignorance of what actually *happens* in torture cases. As we have seen, many theorists defend the view that torture is permissible in cases where there will be no long-term damage to those who are tortured. The thought that there are such cases—or, at any rate, that there are enough that are worthy of comment—seems to evidence a lack of familiarity with the available literature. One of the hallmark features of torture is that *it stays with you*. Regarding torture as an event that can occur and then be complete within a few weeks is to misunderstand the very nature of torture, as well as the kind of trauma that it produces in the bodies and minds of torture survivors. It is our contention that a careful analysis of the phenomenology of torture will go a long way to countering the view that torture is something one can undergo and be done with. Once this view is revealed to be untenable, we will then be in a unique position to identify an essential wrong-making feature of torture: its reliance on obliterating agency by turning agency against itself.

Many of the arguments in favor of torture, for whatever reason, rely on a series of illusions about the nature of torture. Among the most persistent of these are illusions about (1) the lasting effects of torture, (2) the comparative badness of torture as compared with death, and (3) the putative equivalence of torture to other forms of coercion or undesired pain.

To understand the phenomenology of torture is to see through each of these illusions. Torture is marked by its relative permanence—a continuing pain that marks the memory of what the body has been through. It is likewise marked by a fundamental change in those who are subjected to it—a change that destroys one's capacity to interact meaningfully and compassionately with others, and hence with one's capacity to be an agent in the properly human sense at all. It is in torture's very nature to be capable of being worse than death, and it is in its nature to be most unlike other forms of pain and coercion. In coercive situations, one knows what is expected, and one knows what is required to end it. Torture offers no such optimism.[1] Our aim in what follows is to see these illusions for what they are. This, in turn, will allow us to understand why torture is inherently destructive of agency, and hence always impermissible.

FIRST ILLUSION: TORTURE HAS NO LASTING EFFECTS

What happens to you here is forever. . . We shall crush you down to the point from which there is no coming back. Things will happen to you from which you could not recover, if you lived a thousand years. Never again will you be capable of ordinary human feeling. Everything will be dead inside you.

O'Brien to Winston, Nineteen Eighty-Four,
George Orwell, 264–265

Orwell's account is anything but fiction. "It is as if the downward slope from power to powerlessness experienced in relation to the perpetrator has ripped apart the victim's ego and world into two or more pieces . . . " (Haenel, 1). This is how Ferdinand Haenel describes the after-effects of the experience of being tortured. The victims of torture he works with in the Berlin Treatment Center all seem, to use a familiar metaphor, "broken." "Many seem to lack drive and vitality, appearing numb and tense, but they can also be excessively irritable and lose all control of themselves as they succumb to rage" (1).

But this is only the beginning of the struggles faced by those who survive torture. The ones who come to the treatment center are at least making the first steps toward reconciliation with the *humane* side of humanity. To even begin recovery requires getting beyond a supremely powerful feeling of utter powerlessness—a feeling that is created by the very thing one wants to be treated *for.* "A positive course of treatment is fundamentally

handicapped by the way in which the omnipotence of the perpetrators and the powerlessness of their victims lives on in the
inner psychic reality of the latter" (Haenel, 8). To even decide to
seek therapeutic treatment is to show immense *progress*, but this
of course is no guarantee of success: psychiatrists burnout, they
become seen as new perpetrators of torture by their patients,
patients refuse further treatment, or become openly hostile to
the therapeutic process.[2]

The predicament of the person tortured is captured well by
Norbert Gurris, also of the Berlin Treatment Center:

> [F]or the victims, torture is unpredictable in a way that is
> unlike anything they have ever known before, and at the same
> time it is unavoidable and usually uncontrollable. For these
> reasons, torture is something that cannot be mastered. The
> almost always unanticipated breakdown of the self, of the
> self's values, leads to the experience of one's own total failure,
> to self-blame, and therefore to overwhelming feelings of
> shame. (Gurris, 29)

The "total failure" found in torture stems not only from the
near-inevitability of betrayal—even when one is entirely innocent of any particular crime—but also from the very relationship one bears to one's own body. As Gurris puts it: "Through
torture, the unity of body and soul (psychosomatic unity) within
the person is significantly and profoundly disturbed" (30).
Indeed, the dignity that we associate with autonomous adult-
hood is decimated by the act of torture. Quoting Gurris yet
again,

> [I]t no longer fits into our familiar maps of thought and eval-
> uation for a grown human being to become completely
> helpless, to cry or beg for mercy, to void the bowels and pass
> urine in the panic of uncontrolled anxiety, to wish simply to
> be killed at last instead of having to vegetate, and to have even
> this last bit of autonomy refused. Under these circumstances,
> naked biological survival can lead the tortured person to
> betray anyone and everything. So after torture the victim
> finds that he is still somehow alive physically but has been
> psychologically destroyed. (Gurris, 31)

These claims are meant as an explanatory device for the actual long-term effects of torture. Whether or not they are literally true is, in certain respects, irrelevant. Regardless of one's meta-psychological preferences, torture leaves persons fundamentally changed—even unrecognizable to their families and friends. No matter what the strength of one's desire to return to what one was is, the body will normally not allow such wishful regression. "The body . . . seems to want to reflect the agony it is living through, its every wound and devastation" (31). "Torture, which attacks and wounds the self, often leads to a permanent condition of very intense excitement and hypervigilance" (33). As the insightful cliché reminds us, one can never go home again.

What, precisely, causes the changes in one's existence? The claim that one is destroyed psychologically must, of course, be understood metaphorically. In a certain respect, to claim this does not answer any particular question. On the contrary, the question appears to be restated within a different vocabulary. *Why* is one psychologically destroyed by torture, and what does it mean to be so destroyed?

These are important questions. Unfortunately, in a certain respect, they must remain unanswered—or, perhaps better put, our answers here must remain as tentative as our confidence in current psychological theories. One interesting (and plausible) claim that has been made is that torture upsets the schema of an agent; that is, it disrupts the basic organizational assumptions about life, humanity, and value that typically allow adults to understand social interaction and navigate the world around them. (For one such list of assumptions, see Janoff-Bulman, 1992; cited in Gurris, 37.) In many instances, this results in familiar cognitive dissonance: the victim of treatment is angered and blames him- or herself for the actions of the torturer; one becomes convinced that it is one's "weakness" that is to be blamed, rather than the deliberate actions of a torturer. Whether or not such cognitive dissonance is dealt with in this way, one comes to think of oneself, and one's relations to others, in very different terms. The "I–thou" relationship, it would seem, is irretrievably altered. In this respect the end of being subjected to torture is only the beginning of an altered life.

This fact—one that is rarely acknowledged in arguments in favor of permitting torture—is made vivid by Jean Amery in his account of his torture in Auschwitz. "Whoever was tortured, stays tortured. Torture is ineradicably burned into him, even when no clinically objective traces can be detected" (Amery, 34). The sense in which this is true, of course, is both physical and psychological. As Wenk-Ansohn has suggested, *"Pain is embodied memory"* (Wenk-Ansohn, 58). Pain is the way a body remembers the traumas that it has undergone. Once again, the exact mechanism through which this occurs is not of crucial importance. There is reason to think that much pain existing in post-traumatic situations is psychosomatic: persons remember the trauma they have undergone viscerally, through the body. But this is not to say that one's psychic life is in any way unaffected: the torturous event lives on in one's body—one knows why the pain persists—and hence refuses to allow a person to move on. One's conscious energies are repeatedly brought back to the event that marked one's "total failure"—the cessation of one's agency that, paradoxically, one was forced to bring about *oneself.*

As in so much else, George Orwell is particularly insightful when it comes to the devastating effects of torture on its victim: "'What happens to you here is *forever*' . . . That was a true word. There were things, your own acts, from which you could not recover. Something was killed in your breast; burnt out, cauterized out" (301). This view has been reiterated many times over. As Amery puts it,

> whoever has succumbed to torture can no longer feel at home in the world. The shame of destruction cannot be erased. Trust in the world, which already collapsed in part at the first blow, but in the end, under torture, fully, will not be regained. (40)
>
> It is still not over. Twenty-two years later I am still dangling over the ground by dislocated arms, panting, and accusing myself. (36)

When one looks at the trauma that is torture, as described by psychiatrists, survivors, and others, it is hardly surprising that many who are tortured beg for death. That this occurs is a deep clue into how we might weigh the moral atrocities of death and torture in relation to one another. But, as we have seen, undergoing instances of torture is hardly the end of the ordeal. As Amery and others have shown, torture survives with the tortured.

In certain respects, it never leaves him. It is thus hardly surprising that Jean Amery, whom we have quoted above, committed suicide some years after having been tortured. He too judged that torture—even the fact of *having been tortured*—was a worse fate than death. His case is hardly exceptional.

SECOND ILLUSION: TORTURE IS NOT AS BAD AS DEATH

Of pain you could wish only one thing: that it should stop. Nothing in the world was so bad as physical pain. In the face of pain there are no heroes.
Winston, Nineteen Eighty-Four, *George Orwell, 246*

In Henry Shue's seminal article, "Torture," we are presented with the following argument:

1. Just-combat killing is a greater harm than torture usually is.
2. Just-combat killing is sometimes morally permissible.
3. Therefore, torture is sometimes morally permissible.

As Shue goes on to argue, of course, the comparison between just-combat killing and torture is infelicitous: the kind of reciprocity that is necessary for just-combat killing is not present in the case of torture, and the person tortured is utterly at the mercy of the torturer. Despite Shue's capable arguments, versions of the argument given above are presented in a number of articles in *defense* of torture. The revised arguments often employ double-effect reasoning, or defenses of reciprocity requirements in detainee treatment. In some cases, the arguments offered simply play the hypothetical game: if torture can save a life, then it is justified. The thought here seems to be that death must be worse than torture, and hence that the trade-off between torture and death always results in deciding to torture.

What is striking about such arguments is the seeming disregard paid to the actual empirical literature. Let us leave aside, for the moment, questions about guilt and innocence. Let us focus instead on the weight that seems to be attributed to death and torture, respectively. Torture, as we have seen, cannot be regarded as an isolated incident without residual effect. The question that must be posed is thus *not* what is to be preferred, torture or death; the question, more honestly, is as follows: what is to be

preferred, an immediate death or torture, followed by the ago-
nizing life of one who has been tortured? Consider some of the
results of torture:

> When Doctors Finn Somnier and Inge Genefke examined
> twenty-four torture survivors an average of 9.5 years after
> their torture (see "Psychotherapy for Victims of Torture,"
> *British Journal of Psychiatry,* 1986, vol. 149), they found 71
> percent had nightmares, 79 percent complained of headaches,
> 79 percent had impaired memory, 75 percent had impaired
> concentration, 75 percent experienced fatigue, 50 percent suf-
> fered from persistent fear and anxiety, 38 percent experienced
> vertigo, 21 percent reported sexual problems, and 13 percent
> tremors or shaking. (Conroy, 179–180)

But this is not the end of the story. These symptoms are often
accompanied by diagnosed physical conditions: "gastroenteritis,
respiratory infections, skin eruptions, and peptic ulcers are common" (180). According to one view (the theory of conversion
disorders), persons who have suffered great trauma "convert"
this trauma, which they are incapable of fully dealing with, into
actual physical ailments (Conroy, 181). As is obvious, the mental
and physical state of one who has been tortured has significant
implications for inter-personal relationships, and hence on one's
ability to function in social and familial settings. This is often
enough to wrench the last meaningful interactions from the lives
of the broken. All that is left to do, it seems, is die.

> One study of Americans held as POWs during World War II
> and the Korean War ("Follow-up Studies of World War II
> and Korean War Prisoners," *American Journal of Epidemio-
> logy,* 92:2, 1970) noted that in the first three years after their
> repatriation, POWs who had been held in Japan showed a 50
> percent increase in deaths over what would be typical of a
> similar group of white American males. Accidents, tuberculo-
> sis, and cirrhosis of the liver were the primary causes of those
> excess deaths. Suicides, though few in number, were about 30
> percent more frequent than in control groups (182).

The question, to reiterate, appears not to be what is worse,
torture or death. Rather, the question is: is death worse than

torture *and* death? The question requires no answer. Torture *is* a kind of death, but one that draws out one's pain and suffering indefinitely. And this pain, moreover, is the very means by which one's agency is dismantled. To anticipate the next section,

> [U]nlike other kinds of unwanted imposition, pain character-istically compromises or undermines the very capacities constitutive of autonomous agency itself. It is almost impossible to reflect, deliberate, or even think straight when one is in agony. When sufficiently intense, pain becomes a person's entire universe and his entire self, crowding out every other aspect of his mental life. Unlike other harms, pain takes its victim's agency apart "from the inside," such that the agent may never be able to reconstitute himself fully. (Sussman, 14)

This is sufficient, it seems, to demonstrate that death is not the greater of two harms. In fact, quite the contrary.

THIRD ILLUSION: TORTURE IS LIKE OTHER USES OF COERCION AND PAIN

In the end the nagging voices broke him down more completely than the boots and fists of the guards. He became simply a mouth that uttered, a hand that signed whatever was demanded of him.
Nineteen Eighty-Four, *George Orwell, 249*

When we think of torture, it is typically of the physical variety. In certain respects, the existence of pain—considered completely apart from interrogation and the power relations involved therein—is only incidental to the existence of torture. Far more important than the pain one feels in one's body is the helplessness that becomes who one is. Being utterly prostrate to another human being is essential to the torture experience, and also to its lasting (and deeply damaging) effects. The very thing that constitutes us—the fact that we are agents capable of exercising our autonomy in the world—is what we are deprived of when we are subjected to torture.

The most famous analysis of torture as a situational relationship, described in terms of the phenomenology of the tortured, is Elaine Scarry's *The Body in Pain*. The phenomenology of torture reveals a feature of (normal) human experience by presenting us with its negation: the respect that we normally (unreflectively) show to other human beings is perspicuous in its absence from the torture situation. One is reduced from agent to mere body—and in the experience of oneself as mere body, one also suffers self-betrayal. Your body simply cannot hold out. Your body—that thing that you *are* in the world, can no longer be relied on to express your agency. Instead, it stands at the whim and fancy of the agency of another.

Part of what is involved in our mundane conception of the human is the richness of our phenomenological lives: the fact that things can have significance for us, and that this significance can be shared. Whether one thinks this significance can be captured in reductive, empiricist terms, or one thinks that a robust phenomenology is required to capture this aspect of lived human experience is inconsequential: thinkers on both sides of this theoretical divide recognize that it is the *depth* of our experience—the manner in which we experience things as being meaning-laden, that marks an important feature of our form of life, our being-in-the-world.

One disturbing feature of torture is that it represents the "unmaking of an agent's world"[3]—the reduction of the phenomenological world of the tortured to a series of procedures and instruments. The everyday significance of ordinary objects takes on a new, twisted significance: the hammer becomes, not simply the piece of equipment that would enable us to complete a project, but the menacing presence that will be used to smash my extremities. Ordinary objects take on extraordinary significance: our world is reduced to the world of the torturer. Pain "unmakes" the world—but worse, it makes us incapable of recognizing ourselves *qua* selves. We are reduced to a single experience, a single feature: our pain. As Elaine Scarry puts it:

> It is the intense pain that destroys a person's self and world, a destruction experienced spatially as either the contraction of the universe down to the immediate vicinity of the body or as the body swelling to fill the entire universe. Intense pain is also language-destroying: as the content of one's world disintegrates, so the content of one's language disintegrates; as the

self disintegrates, so that which would express and project the self is robbed of its source and subject. (35)

The view we find in Scarry's work is tremendously insightful. It reveals to us what is involved in the phenomenology of (part of) torture: a reduction of significance and self to a singularity. The agent's experience of time is made into the awareness only of the immediate—of the pain felt by one and forced by another.

And here we can see once again that pain—though effective in reducing our experience to a single point—to the pain we feel— is actually overshadowed by the other features of torture. As Scarry explicitly notes, torture has two fundamental aspects: (1) a primary physical act, and (2) a primary verbal act. The verbal act consists of question and answer (35). We cannot understand (most forms of) torture without acknowledging that the mere presence of pain is *not* co-extensive with it. Torture is likewise *not* simply pain plus questioning. On the contrary, "the interrogation does not stand outside an episode of torture as its motive or justification: it is internal to the structure of torture, exists there because of its intimate connections to and interactions with the physical pain" (29). Pain and interrogation are experienced as opposites. "For the torturers, the sheer and simple fact of human agony is made invisible, and the moral fact of inflicting that agony is made neutral by the feigned urgency and significance of the question" (29). In this context, one's body overtakes everything else ("the claims of the body utterly nullify the claims of the world" [33]). When intense physical pain is dispensed amid a torrent of questions, one experiences pain and question as interwoven—and the way that such things might fit into a life becomes utterly inconceivable: "the absence of pain is the presence of world; the presence of pain is the absence of world" (37).

As the prisoner's world shrinks, the torturer's world grows in size and significance. This, Scarry notes, constitutes a falsification of the pain of the tortured—it "objectifies one crucial aspect of pain in order to falsify all other aspects" (37). The mundane objects that litter our lives are turned against us: the room itself is "converted into another weapon" (40). The floor, the chair, the bed, even medicine become instruments through which our agency is contorted, and through which we are led to experience the inhumanity of our fellow human beings.

The force of this should not be downplayed. Artifacts are the very essence of the human—the very thing through which matter is made into meaning, as Ernest Becker once put it.[4] In this respect, the use of places of dwelling as designated places where agency will be stripped away—and use of pieces of material culture to *annihilate* the culture within one, if only temporarily—are among the most sinister of atrocities. The very things that represent the achievements of humanity materially—tools, artifacts, spaces of communal dwelling—are turned into the instruments of destruction of the human.

> Through the torturer's language, his actions, and the physical setting, the world is brought to the prisoner in three rings: the random technological and cultural embodiments of civilization overarch the two primary social institutions of medicine and law, which in turn overarch the basic unit of shelter, the room. Just as the prisoner's confession makes visible the contraction and closing in of his universe, so the torturer reenacts this world collapse. Civilization is brought to the prisoner and in his presence annihilated in the very process by which it is being made to annihilate him. (Scarry, 44)

As should be clear, torture is, in many ways, the antonym of civilization. It is the thing that we leave behind among the savages when we join into communities, opting to live in trust and mutual respect. To torture is to subject someone to the most animalistic kind of existence—to reveal to one what the absence of civilization might mean, and to do so in a way that makes civilization—in its most robust sense—unattainable for the future.

It is at this point that we can begin to see how distinct torture is from simple coercion, on the one hand, and other kinds of pain, on the other. David Sussman has compellingly argued that the wrong-making feature of torture lies in its dual nature as (1) painful, and (2) involving a social setting of utter hopelessness. Importantly, Sussman contends that *both* of these things must be present for us to felicitously call something "torture."

This enables Sussman to distinguish torture from mere coercion, on the one hand, and brain-washing, on the other.

> Torture should be distinguished from both coercion and brain-washing, even though all three may often overlap in particular cases. What is distinctive about torture is that it aims to manipulate its victims through their own responses, as agents, to the felt experience of their affects and emotions in a context of dependence, vulnerability, and disorientation. Coercion, in contrast, need only exploit the agent's rational responses to the cognitive content of these feelings. The coercer tries to influence his victims through their own appreciation of their reasons for action . . . Coercion, as a kind of hard bargaining by means of threats, involves too direct an appeal to its victim's rationality to count as torture. (9)

In this respect, coercion is *more* respectful of an agent than torture, as coercion relies on an agent's rational capabilities in a way that torture does not. Although the torturer might, in some cases, appeal to the capacities of an agent in order to get information, this is intermingled with agency-crushing action. "What the torturer does is to take his victim's pain, and through it his victim's body, and make it begin to express the torturer's will" (Sussman, 21). Moreover, the verbal portion of the torture situation involves a consistent deception: rather than simply black-mailing or hard-bargaining with a person, the torturer aims to dismantle the subject's world through questioning that is often simply irrational (recall our discussion of the aim to 'regress' detainees in torture situations by destroying their sense of order). For the torturer, unlike the coercer, nothing is sacred.

> [T]he most intimate and private parts of a victim's life and body become publicly available tools for the torturer to exploit as he will. The victim is completely exposed, while the torturer is free to conceal anything he likes, even those things to which a victim clearly has a right and a profound interest . . . the asymmetry of power, knowledge, and prerogative is absolute: the victim is in a position of complete vulnerability and exposure, the torturer in one of perfect control and inscrutability. (Sussman, 7)

Torture is thus *not* like coercion, nor is it like an average instance of pain. It is, as we have persistently seen, a uniquely repulsive phenomenon.

TORTURE AND THE PHENOMENOLOGY OF DIGNITY

Dispelling the above illusions enables us to take a closer look at one of the essential (perhaps *the* essential) wrong-making features of torture. As we have seen, the tortured is stripped of dignity—their very agency is turned against them—and they become a mere puppet in the hands of another agent. The tortured is reduced to mere biological function, and then the very biological functions that constitute one's minimal, animal being are turned against one.

The most famous defense of the inalienable dignity of human beings is certainly found in Kant. One need not accept Kant's elaborate ethical theory to accept one of its basic features—arguably the very feature that justifies Kant's assertion that he is merely articulating common knowledge about the nature of morality. Kant maintains, as is well known, that an essential feature of morality is treating humanity, wherever it is found, as an end-in-itself—as something with *dignity* rather than *price*.

In the *Groundwork for the Metaphysics of Morals,* Kant puts this point in the form of an imperative: "*So act that you use humanity, whether in your own person or in the person of any other, always at the same time as an end, never merely as a means*" (4:429). In the *Critique of Practical Reason,* Kant elaborates this constitutive principle of morality as follows:

[A] human being alone, and with him every rational creature, is an *end-in-itself* . . . such a being is not to be subjected to any purpose that is not possible in accordance with a law that could arise from the will of the affected [*leidenden*] subject himself; hence this subject is to be used never merely as a means but as at the same time an end. (5:87)

It is unclear how precisely to establish the validity of this particular claim. Kant himself offers an argument, though it has not persuaded many who did not already accept the dignity of humanity. The argument runs (roughly) as follows: as agents, we value those things that enable us to achieve our (subjective) wants. Thus, at this moment, we value the computer that enables us to write this book. We value this precisely because it enables us to achieve our goals. Now, the one thing above all else that enables us to achieve our goals is our agency *as such.* If I were not an agent, I would be unable to even *decide* to co-author the current text. Thus, it appears, my agency must be valued if anything at all is. When we further investigate this value, we notice that it is not *my* agency *per se* that is valued, but agency in itself. Analogously, when I chew food, I value teeth—the ones I have in my head, to be sure, but I am not valuing the fact that they are *mine.* If, by some strange turn of events, the teeth I used to chew my food belonged to someone else, I would value them all the same. Likewise with agency. What is important is that I am an agent, *not* that the agency I embody is *mine.* If, by some strange turn of events, I discovered that my agency was actually on lease from some higher being, I would value it all the same. This shows, Kant contends, that *if we value anything at all* we are committed to valuing agency *as such*—and this obviously includes the agency of others.

This argument tends to either totally convince or leave totally unmoved those who encounter it. The problem with the argument seems to be that it relies on a move from self-regarding interests to other-regarding interests in one swift move. The contentious claim, of course, lies in the view that what we value is *agency itself* rather than *my particular* agency. While I do value agency as such, it seems like a stretch to say that the agency I value is something I possess indifferently. It *matters,* after all, that *I possess* agency—even if what I value is "agency" in some general sense (which, so far as it goes, seems rather compelling). Left to choose between agency as possessed by me and agency as possessed by another, the value that I maintain *toward* agency would certainly not yield a judgment of indifference. If this is so, it is at least puzzling how I get from valuing agency *in me* (even if it is not "mine" per se) to valuing agency *in others.*

The mistake in the argument (at least as so far discussed) lies in the idea that we begin by only valuing ourselves and *then* move to valuing others. As a matter of psychological development, this might well be true; as a claim about the ontology of value, however, it is false. Kant's attempt, here as elsewhere, is to reconstruct through reason a commitment that we *already* have, not to *establish* this commitment (recall that this argument occurs in the *Groundwork,* where Kant claims to be engaged in an analytic process rather than a synthetic one). Rather than attempting to reconstruct the Kantian position, let's turn instead to the claim that the dignity of human beings is something to which all agents are in some sense committed.[5]

The claim that all agents recognize, at some level, the dignity of humanity is a remarkably difficult one to establish through argument. Its initial plausibility is met with continuous counter-example: we must manage to explain those cases where human beings are treated as mere things, where they are disrespected either by other individuals or by institutions as a whole. And one does not have to look far to find such instances of the inhumanity of humanity.

If the claim about the recognition of the dignity of others is correct, though, then such counter examples are no more troubling for this account than mirages are for an account of vision: in any perceptual faculty we can make mistakes. Indeed, there are certain circumstances where it is even *expected* that we will make mistakes. In crowds of persons, it is common for persons to hear their own names called. In periods of intense sensory deprivation, the mind will construct its own "sensory" stimuli to satisfy what we might call its "world hunger." We expect such illusory experiences to emerge given the structure of experience and the parameters of human psychology. Thus, if there is a basic perception of the dignity of persons, we will likewise expect that this perception, under certain circumstances, will be compromised.

As we can see, then, the view that there is a basic phenomenology of respect is not defeated by the claim that there are instances where human beings suffer moral blind spots. This, however, does very little to actually *justify* the claim that our recognition of the respect owed to others is basic. To defend this view requires, in our estimate, a defense of the idea that there are moral primitives—that is, that there are true value assertions that do not admit of justification in terms of even more basic value statements. Any attempt to offer reasons for such moral primitives will in effect restate those primitives in paraphrase rather than offering actual inferential support. Such paraphrase, of course, is incredibly useful in a wide range of contexts. In cases where mutual understanding has not been achieved, paraphrase is the bridge over linguistic confusion. Likewise, when we are questioned about basic value assertions (like "cruelty is wrong"), the most we can do is paraphrase these assertions in a way that might make them more comprehensible ("it is wrong to cause unnecessary pain"). The two sentences, in cases like this, stand in a relationship of clarification rather than justification. It is this that we have in mind when we speak of "moral primitives": they are value assertions that can be (perhaps infinitely) paraphrased, but which cannot be justified by appeal to more basic value assertions.

The reason such inferential chains cannot be established, in essence, is that no chain of inference will be more secure than that which is meant to be justified by the chain of inference. This is an important point, and should not be glossed over too quickly. It is always possible to construct arguments with any particular sentence as a conclusion. This syntactical possibility, however, does not amount to justifying a proposition through inference. It is fairly easy to construct arguments with obvious conclusions and impossibly complicated premises. The ability to do this has little bearing on the epistemic status of *particular* propositions. Thus, even if the proposition "cruelty is wrong" resulted from a complex argument, the argument itself would not yield anything like epistemic gain through inference, as the chain of premises leading to the conclusion would be less secure than the conclusion itself.[6]

None of this yet demonstrates that there are moral primitives, nor that respect for persons is such a primitive. What it does do, however, is to establish an approach to establishing such a primitive. Before spelling out this argument, a few more preliminary assumptions need to be articulated: first, in speaking of the respect owed to human beings, we are explicitly avoiding marginal cases. We are specifically talking about *persons,* not those entities that happen to be genetically human, or those that have the capacity to become persons. It *might* be the case that we owe respect to fetuses, the brain-dead, and higher-order primates. These positions are all compatible with the view that respect for persons is basic. These views are not, however, entailed by the view we defend. Second, we will assume that there are at least some moral truths. Defending this claim is well beyond the scope of this book—and, indeed, is even *presupposed* by the book—so we will not bother to defend this view here.

It is our contention that respect for persons is a moral primitive. If this is correct, it will turn out that there are no arguments available for this claim that are more secure than the claim itself. The only possible arguments that might justify this conclusion would involve picking out the morally salient features of persons as the things that merit respect, and then deducing from this the general view that persons are worthy of our respect. Thus, one might contend that it is not personhood per se, but *rationality,* which warrants our respect. It could then be deduced that all persons are rational to a certain degree, and hence are worthy of our respect.

There are two responses to this argument that are worth making. The first response is as follows: if rationality is what we respect, and the degree of rationality differs from person to person, it would appear that the dignity of persons would also have to vary. While this might be true, it seems to conflict with a strong moral intuition that persons are *equally worthy* of respect (morally speaking), regardless of how developed their rational capacities are. Einstein deserves no more *moral* respect than does Forrest Gump.[7]

A second response—and one that is in our view more powerful—might run as follows: It is virtually impossible to imagine a person that had no rational abilities: to be a person means minimally to be able to understand yourself existing across time, executing plans and making decisions based on what has transpired. To do such things obviously involves minimal rationality. If it is true that all persons are to a certain degree rational, and if it is true that all rational creatures admit of some of the minimal standards of personhood, then it is not clear that the concepts of "rationality" and "personhood" can actually come apart in any significant sense. That is, to speak of rationality as possessing a dignity may well be a way of *paraphrasing* the claim that *persons* are worthy of respect. Thus, the attempt to deduce the claim that "persons are worthy of respect" from the claim that "those with rationality are worthy of respect" is to deduce a truism from a truism—and hence to deduce nothing at all. The same analysis holds of other particular features of personhood, it seems: autonomy seems as central to personhood as does anything else, at least if this is understood in a minimalist sense. Thus, we can conclude that respect for persons is a morally primitive notion, as it cannot be deduced from anything more certain than the proposition itself is.

An obvious objection needs to be met here. One reason there might be no arguments for the view that all persons are owed respect is that the view is *false*. There is no knock-down argument to defeat this view. All we can do, at this point, is to highlight some features of our experience that make clear that we in fact *do* regard persons as worthy of respect. One can be skeptical about such experiences, of course, if one is a skeptic about morality in general—a view we will not here address.[8] It is our view, however, that the demands made on us in everyday experience are sufficiently pervasive to justify the view that we do in fact experience other persons as demanding our respect. This sentiment has been captured in a number of authors, not the least of whom is Levinas: "the face opens the primordial discourse whose first word is obligation, which no 'interiority' permits avoiding" (201).[9] To see another human being is to see *that* one is obligated—it is to see an "infinity" that is utterly beyond our own subjectivity. "This infinity, stronger than murder, already resists us in his face, is his face, is the primordial *expression,* is the first word: 'you shall not commit murder'" (199).

What Levinas colorfully captures is also what Kant clearly saw: to be a moral agent just means to acknowledge the ability of other agents to make demands on you. This, it seems to us, partially constitutes what is involved in respecting a person. We can regard respect for persons as a moral primitive, though, not just because it is a basic feature of experience, but because it cannot be deduced from anything more epistemically secure than it itself is. This justifies the view that persons are indeed owed a respect in *all* circumstances. As such, respect for other persons is a categorical imperative, and utterly at odds with the practice of torture.

DIGNITY, CONSENT, AND TORTURE: A CONCLUDING OBJECTION

Despite a compelling experience of the dignity of others, there are those who will respond that the dignity of which we speak might be compatible with torture. Respecting agents, in certain cases, might actually *warrant* torturing them—at least so some might argue. Kant himself suggested that respect for an agent might in some cases merit *killing* that agent. If this is so, why might someone not argue that respect is perfectly compatible with torture?

As Kant claims in the *Metaphysics of Morals,* "the *right to punish* is the right a ruler has against a subject to inflict pain upon him because of his having committed a crime" (6:331). Such a punishment, Kant insists, is entirely compatible with respecting the agent who has committed a crime—indeed, it is *required* insofar as the criminal is an autonomous agent deserving of our respect: "every murderer—anyone who commits murder, orders it, or is an accomplice in it—must suffer death; this is what justice, as the idea of judicial authority, wills in accordance with universal laws that are grounded *a priori*" (6:333). Importantly, the authority to impose a death penalty on a subject is granted to a ruler *by the subject.* As Kant insists, the authority of law stems from *homo noumenon*—from the most rational and autonomous part of us. When one decides to commit a capital offense, their course of action requires our respect—they have opted to violate the law. Respecting the wishes of the agent involves carrying out the appropriate punishments when and if that agent is caught.

An analogous argument might be attempted by those who would defend torture—one that is worth considering in some detail. If persons violate laws—the laws of war, for example— these persons are essentially consenting to be treated in ways that do not fall under the rules of war. Reciprocity, it has sometimes been argued,[10] is an essential part of the Geneva Conventions. When persons do not act in accordance with these accords, they are thereby consenting to not be treated themselves as falling under these accords. Thus, the argument goes, those who defy standard rules of war (avoiding killing innocent civilians, wearing uniforms, openly displaying arms, no torture, etc.) can be respected only by not *applying* those same rules of war to them. Consider this argument in a more schematic form:[11]

1. We should respect human agents, which entails respecting their choices.
2. If an agent chooses x, knowing that x can result in y, then an agent willingly accepts y.

3. If an agent knows that crime x will result in punishment y, that agent willingly accepts the risk of y.
4. Therefore, respecting an agent entails punishing that agent when she commits a crime.

The obvious problem with this argument is that premise two is false. Consider a parallel case: Let's say that I have been enslaved in a country that supports slavery. I decide that I cannot accept living in such conditions. I happen to know that the punishment for those slaves who escape from bondage is a severe beating, followed by a return to slavery. If the second premise of the above argument is true, then by choosing to escape from slavery, I am also willingly accepting my future slavery. As is obvious, this is absurd. The entire *point* of escaping from slavery is to *reject* this unjust practice. To say that by rejecting it one is in fact accepting it in the future is nonsense.

To be fair to Kant, he too would likely reject the second premise—at least in its current form. Kant would insist that an agent who chooses x only (rationally) accept y insofar as y is a *justifiable* result of x. In other words, the argument works only when we are dealing with *just laws.* If I murder someone, and the death penalty is *in fact* a just punishment, then I cannot thereby claim that I have not also committed myself to the punishment insofar as I autonomously chose an action *punishable* by death. This point, though, borders on the tautologous. *Of course* respecting an agent's choice involves carrying out the fully warranted consequences of that choice. But notice that this argument *cannot* be used to establish that a particular punishment is just or unjust. To attempt to do so would be to beg the question.

And it is here that we see why any argument attempting to use the above (roughly Kantian) argument in establishing the justice of torture will fail. Arguments from consent, of the form given above, cannot *establish* the justice of anything. They cannot do this precisely because such arguments work only if we can presume the justice of the punishments/consequences being considered. Thus, we are entitled to reject the (confused) view that respecting the dignity of an agent might in certain instances involve carrying out torture on that agent. Given that this line of argument has been closed off, it is clear that respecting the dignity of a person requires respecting their agency. As we have seen, *every instance* of torture is about as far removed from respect as one can get. It reduces one to the merely animal, often in the name of acquiring information, and then turns even one's animal agency against one. The consequences of the total failure experienced in torture leaves one destroyed, often in such a way that a human life is no longer possible. One's body becomes a constant reminder of the lows to which humanity may sink; one's crushed psyche becomes incapable of normal, loving relationships. All that is left to do, in essence, is to die.

There will likely be a temptation, at this point, for those who would like to defend torture to revert to utilitarian reasoning of the ticking-bomb variety. The cases one attempts to construct along these lines, however, we have demonstrated to be fallacious (Chapter Two). Thus, even if we cannot establish that the dignity of an agent is *never* to be violated (a position we embrace), we *have* demonstrated that there are no instances of torture where such a violation is permissible.

CHAPTER FOUR

THE DRAMATURGICAL MODEL OF TORTURE

INTERROGATION'S IMMORALITY PLAY

Torture is theatrical. When our mind wanders the hallways conjured by the term, the violence we envision is as graphic as anything we are likely ever to encounter. We are at once both horrified and entertained by it. It's no surprise that museums devoted to torture are both prolific and successful. There is even a recent genre of movie which critics have dubbed "torture porn." Some of these movies, in turn, have generated their own gruesome, blood-soaked franchises. In this same tradition, thought experiments which involve it are pure spectacle. Much like Roman "bread and circuses," the contemplation of torture and its illusory moral permissibility appeals to our basest desires, seductively convinces us of our safety and moral superiority (we can act as the barbarian against the barbarian, should it save the civilized), and it distracts us from cases of actual torture. While theatrical torture entices and entertains us as we watch Jack Bauer go to work torturing an enemy operative for the greater good, real torture moves quietly, dull and unchecked.

Modern torture is often decidedly (and even intentionally) non-graphic. Instead of hammers, scalpels, drills, iron maidens, stretching racks, and pliers, a torturer's work may be done with an adjusted schedule, a persistent noise, lack of sleep, a change in diet, an awkward position, a closed fist, or a bended knee. For those who think about torture through the thought experiment of the spectacle of the ticking bomb, modern torture might even disappoint.

This undeniable theatrical element of torture invites, for the purposes of this investigation, a third framework through which to assess the practice. In our view, the philosopher's penchant for the armchair has perhaps moved the ethical analysis of torture away from the realm of the real to the realm of the artificial.

In the United States' current history, torture is more likely to be committed by an impressionable, love-struck private than it is by a sociopathic monster. That the scandal generated by the abuse at Abu Ghraib prison was generated by photographs of prison guards actually *posing* for the camera comes as no surprise to many social psychologists who, when they saw that the scene was ripe, may have in fact *predicted* such abuse. Those who were eventually found guilty of abusing those who they considered beneath them understood that they were actors in a drama larger than themselves. As the photos coldly testify, they were happy to play their roles.

The spectacle of torture naturally invites metaphors inspired by drama. We might easily think of a torture dungeon as a stage, the torturer and victims as the actors, and the instruments of pain and large, mysterious dossiers as props. Each actor has his specific role and boundaries for improvisation. The torturer is to be mute to the cries of his fellow actor. He is to be creative, but cold. The victim is to cry out, and his role—which he takes very seriously—demands that he yield no information. Each actor must prepare for the part backstage. The torturer might practice his grimace and his questions in front of a mirror. He has to sharpen his tools and lay them out for his counterpart to see. Perhaps he dims the lights and draws the curtains; like any actor he must prepare for his performance. The victim, for his part, might in his back-stage moments remind himself of his comrades or tell himself a story about courage or perseverance, hoping that he won't make any mistakes. Such dramatic observations are also made by Pericles Korovessis, an actor and political activist, of his own torturers:

> Things were beginning to get serious. I got up from the chair and stepped backwards into the corner by the radiator. The madman with the chair came towards me like a lion-tamer. I noticed he was smiling. It seemed rather as if he was acting. He hit me twice with the chair. He kept repeating the same thing. The blows were restrained. He had a twinkle in his eye. I was convinced he was acting. It's my job, after all.
>
> This was followed by the Second Act. Some other *haifes* came in and grabbed the "madman." Somebody asked me if I was still alive. "You're lucky he didn't chuck you out of the

window," added someone else. The madman was still roaring his head off. "I've got him now. Let me get my revenge." They calmed him down, saying it couldn't possibly be me, as I must have been a very small child in '44. The madman wouldn't have it. He wanted his revenge, and was not interested in rational arguments. If I wasn't the one, I had a Communist face and was going to pay for it. They kept saying, "Calm down, Mítsos old feller," but it didn't have any effect. Next came an appearance from Spanós, who said, "Be quiet, lads;" and the lads, with the madman at their head, answered, "Right, Mr. Superior," and went out quietly, almost civilized, like actors who take a bow and disappear into the wings. (Korovessis, 76)

The utility of the metaphor of the stage does not collapse when we are asked to move away from the philosopher's imagined spectacle and think about actual cases of torture. In our opinion, this metaphor helps us get a clearer grasp of certain ethical elements of modern torture that other models may easily overlook. Indeed, thinking about human interaction in general is helpfully illuminated by importing the dramatic metaphor into the domain of the social sciences.

Jauques' now well-worn remark in Shakespeare's "As You Like It" that "All the world's a stage, And all the men and women merely players: They have their exits and their entrances; And one man in his time plays many parts,"[1] certainly must have resonated with sixteenth-century audiences as well as it does with today's. In the middle of the twentieth century, the similarities between an actor's on-stage performances and private individuals' attempts to project and maintain a public image were also not lost on social psychologists.

In Sociology, as soon as the dramaturgical perspective entered the scene, it quickly became an in-vogue perspective for illuminating and studying human social interaction. The dramaturgical perspective, though, certainly is not a unified field. It has its disagreements—epistemological, ontological, metaphysical and methodological—like any respectable discipline. Nevertheless, as a method for surveying and studying that most curious of beasts—the human being, and all the drama brought with it—it reaps ample analytical reward. The roots of dramaturgical analysis run deep in the fertile soil of the sociological perspective of symbolic interactionism. Symbolic interactionism has as its theoretical muse the pragmatism of George Herbert Mead—though this inspiration can perhaps be traced back even into the work of the American pragmatist philosophers: Dewey, James, and Pierce. Symbolic interactionism as an approach to sociological analysis was first championed and fashioned by Mead's student, Herbert Blumer, at the University of Chicago. While Blumer's integration of the work of the American pragmatists and the writings of the sociologists William Thomas and Charles Colley made him the perspective's godfather, the brilliance, lucidity, and humanity found in Erving Goffman's writings have made him the perspective's most notable celebrity.

In *Symbolic Interactionism: Perspective and Method*, Blumer introduces his perspective in this way:

> Symbolic interactionism rests in the last analysis on three simple premises. The first premise is that human beings act toward things on the basis of the meanings that things have for them. Such things include everything that the human being may note in his world—physical objects, such as trees or chairs; other human beings, such as a mother or a store clerk; categories of human beings, such as friends or enemies; institutions, as a school or a government; guiding ideals, such as individual independence or honesty; activities of others, such as their commands or requests; and such situations as an individual encounters in his daily life. The second premise is that the meaning of such things is derived from, or arises out of, the social interaction that one has with one's fellows. The third premise is that these meanings are handled in, and modified through, an interpretive process used by the person in dealing with the things he encounters. (Blumer, 2)

For Blumer, *meaning* was an in-eliminable element in the explanation of social action. Meanings are a product and consequence of the process of social interaction. Moreover, included in the category of meaning are situational definitions, ascriptions of reality, and the self itself.

One of Goffman's research projects throughout his career was an analysis of what he called the interaction order. He was fascinated by one key element of social life: face-to-face interaction. "[I]t is in social situations," he writes in *Gender Advertisements*,

> that individuals can communicate in the fullest sense of the term, and it is only in them that individuals can coerce one another, assault one another, importune one another gesturally, give physical comfort, and so forth. Moreover, it is in social situations that most of the world's work gets done. (6)

Goffman's analysis of interaction takes nourishment from symbolic interactionism's Meadian roots. The capacity for taking the perspective—the role—of the other was, for Mead, essential for understanding how the self developed.

Goffman's digestion of this Meadian nutrient is nicely exhibited in his explosive arrival on the sociological scene:

> When an individual enters the presence of others, they commonly seek to acquire information about him or to bring into play information about him already possessed. They will be interested in his general socio-economic status, his conception of self, his attitude toward them, his competence, his trustworthiness, etc. Although some of this information seems to be sought almost as an end in itself, there are usually quite practical reasons for acquiring it. Information about the individual helps to define the situation, enabling others to know in advance what he will expect of them and what they may expect of him. Informed in these ways, the others will know how best to act in order to call forth a desired response from him. (Goffman, *Presentation of Self,* 1)

Goffman spent the remainder of his career exploring, in myriad situations, the ways in which human beings monitor, manage, and manipulate their co-presence with others. Dramaturgy became the dominant metaphor that Goffman appealed to for revealing the performative aspect of social interaction. It was these metaphors, lifted from the theater, that he appealed to again and again to undertake his ethnology of the self.[2]

On its face, however, conceiving human action in a dramaturgical vocabulary appears to conflict in principle to the aim of normative ethical exploration. There is, we think, apparent friction for at least three reasons. The first is the dramaturgical view of the self as meaning which is itself a consequence of social interaction, the second is the corresponding view of motive, and the final is an overall ethical assessment of the dramaturgical standpoint.

Perhaps the most fundamental aspect of the dramaturgical self, as morality is concerned, is the fact that the self is conceived not as an object but rather as a meaning. The self is a *consequence*, not an antecedent, of human interaction. It is, as Goffman wrote:

> In analyzing the self then we are drawn from its possessor, from the person who will profit or lose most by it, for he and his body merely provide the peg on which something of a collaborative manufacture will be hung for a time. And the means for producing and maintaining selves do not reside inside the peg; in fact these means are often bolted down in social establishments. There will be a back region with its tools for shaping the body, and a front region with its fixed props. There will be a team of persons whose activity on stage in conjunction with available props will constitute the scene from which the performed character's self will emerge, and another team, the audience, whose interpretive activity will be necessary for this emergence. The self is a product of all these arrangements, and in all of its parts bears the marks of this genesis. (*Presentation of Self*, 253)

The self is built upon a process of cooperative inter-activity. It is an inherently relational concept that requires others as a validating audience, not just conceptually, but actually. While one's own performances outline the self, the individual "must rely on others to complete the picture" (Goffman, "Deference and Demeanor", 58).

The self is produced, not merely presented, in symbolic interactions, which for Goffman were also largely ritualistic in their nature. When others' expressive behavior does not agree with one's own attempts at self presentation, one's own self is largely re-shaped. He writes at the end of *The Presentation of Self in Everyday Life*:

> In this report the performed self was seen as some kind of image, usually creditable, which the individual on stage and

in character effectively attempts to induce others to hold in regard to him. While this image is entertained *concerning* the individual, so that a self is imputed to him, this self itself does not derive from its possessor, but from the whole scene of his action, being generated by that attribute of local events which renders them interpretable by witnesses. A correctly staged and performed scene leads the audience to impute a self to a performed character, but this imputation—this self—is a *product* of a scene that comes off, and is not a *cause* of it. (253)

For morality's sake, this conception of the self has obvious consequences. Instead of one's actions *displaying* or following from a self's internal structure or characteristics, characteristics result from one's immersion in performance. There is, then, nothing *there* to which a moral trait or virtue can attach itself, display, or be a consequence of. Indeed, the very moral category of *character* must, on this model, be dramatically reassessed. There is no deeper structure to the self other than one's doings—indeed, selves are only possibilities until they are acted and accepted before and by audiences.

According to the dramaturgical model, the conception of a *true* or *real* self is nonsensical. Moreover, we can display different selves in different situations. In fact, like any good stage performer, one typically has a repertoire of many selves. So we are, according to the dramaturgist, different selves in different relationships and in different scenes. Nevertheless, a sense of continuity or unity is demanded of these different selves. I cannot be the wise man in one scene while also the buffoon in another—those roles are so different and perceived as in tension, that they strain credulity for any competent audience. Thus our range of self-presentations will often be limited.

Connected to the dramaturgical understanding of self is a concern with motivation. Dramaturgical analysis is silent as to the origin of human activity—indeed, the very issue is re-cast.

Motives are not viewed as forces that stir people to act. Instead, motives are seen as expressive communications, both verbal and nonverbal, that are utilized in certain encounters to justify or rationalize the conduct of those persons in those situations. In this sense, motives do not compel human

action—they enable it. The right motive may keep an interaction going; its absence may contribute to the collapse of
the situation. Motives are best understood in the same way
that every other dramaturgical concept is—as elements in
social interaction not as phenomena that reside in individuals, societies, or cultures. (Brisset and Edgley, 22)

Motives play a functional role in maintaining an image of the
self to others. They link "the question of who one is with the
question of what one is doing" (Brisset and Edgley, 22). Indeed,
as Edgley and Brisset recognize, questions about one's motives
are often tackled by simply stating who one is. This assessment of
motive is quite starkly contrasted with philosophical intuitions of
our own moral psychology. We think of the virtuous among us
as pushed by the right desires or pulled by universalizable reasons. However, according to the dramaturgical perspective, to be
motivated, then, is simply to be held responsible for potentially
communicating with others about one's behavior.

The fundamental story is not an inner one involving one's
"true" motives, desires, or picture of the good. Rather, the fundamental fact—and here again dramaturgy's Meadian roots are
exposed—is that people act. Instead of our day's work being
incited by rational choice and reasoned deliberation, our actions
are rote and largely habitual. As far as our activity is concerned,
this model stipulates that we (whatever, if anything, that might
be) are mostly passengers, not drivers. On those occasions when
our activity is interrupted, we account for ourselves to a particular audience in a rationalizing manner for a particular purpose (which is itself often connected to a project of impression
management and construction). This story of our moral psychology—or lack thereof—seems disagreeable, to say the least,
to those philosophers who wish for a moral realism with any
ontological teeth.

In addition to these concerns, there have been attacks leveled
against the perspective as a whole. Don Martindale wrote in *The
Nature and Types of Sociological Theory* that the dramaturgist's
view of civilization

is largely an ever-changing panorama of fabrication in which
the most basic stratification is between the deceivers and the

> deceived and the self in the end always remains . . . an amoral merchant of morality ever intent on the pillage of others or the avoidance of their pillage of him . . . (364)

The attack seems to distill into a Machiavellian picture of the perspective as one that promotes the view that the human animal is merely a strategic, deceiving beast which presents a picture of the self and situation that it hopes others will buy for its own strategic purposes.

Despite these initial doubts, the dramaturgical perspective is particularly favorable for illuminating some moral aspects of human conduct that might otherwise remain hidden. In particular, we think that helpful insights can be teased from Goffman's analysis in particular that can be brought to bear on the moral aspects of military interrogation—which in recent history has been the antecedent for detainee treatment which has been tantamount to torture.

First, unlike much other social psychology, the dramaturgical perspective does not view human beings on a strongly deterministic model. In discussing the dramaturgical perspective, Edgley and Brisset remark as follows:

> [H]umans, by virtue of their expressiveness, are empowered to negotiate their meanings in situations with similarly empowered others. The dignity of humans, in fact, resides in such empowerment. Rather than construing humans as objects that at most deflect, filter and interpret the forces that act on them, dramaturgy asserts the power of human beings as subjects of their destiny. In fact, matters of power, influence, and control are not viewed as unitary, distinguishable forces at all but rather as meanings that emerge out of interaction itself. (3)

The dramaturgist's stock in trade is the fact that all human action, whether we want it to be or not, is expressive. Much like Sartre's remark that man is "condemned to freedom" the dramaturgist sentences us to be "condemned to expression." For Goffman our dramaturgical awareness, the recognition that our acts express both intentionally and unintentionally—in Goffman's terms, that our expressive messages are both "given" and "given off," is what leads us to manipulate our own messages while at the same time analyzing and interpreting those messages in others. But the condemnation of expression does not only apply to our physical doings, it also applies of course to our sayings. According to this model, our verbal behavior should also be understood as contributing to our construction and maintenance of self (i.e. impressing a sense of self on others). What we *say*, and how others *respond*, are fundamentally essential types of social interaction. Goffman himself observes that "we spend most of our time not engaged in giving information but in giving shows" (*Frame Analysis*, 511).

For Goffman, our normal talk constitutes not only bald statements of fact; talk is also much about recounting, about "story telling."

> The argument that much of talk consists of replayings and that these make no sense unless some form of storyteller's suspense can be maintained shows the close relevance of frame—indeed, the close relevance of dramaturgy—for the organization of talk. (Chriss, 558)

As speakers, we represent ourselves as the protagonists in dramatic events. As James Chriss observes, "In effect, we each have at our disposal a wide array of naturally occurring dramatic personae from which to draw in normal everyday speech, and this is not alarming" (558).

Successful dramaturgical interaction also requires certain antecedents which have a quasi-moral status. For one, performing a role requires an ability to understand the consequences and effects of those actions on others. Performing a role thus demands taking, at the same time, the perspective of the audience. Even if it is true that many of our performances are aimed at promoting our own selfish goals (this is the perception which seems to motivate the critics), even these performances require taking the role of the other. Joel Charon writes,

> *Those who abuse* power, abuse children, abuse women, abuse employees, abuse customers are all examples of people who need not understand at least superficially the perspective of those they abuse. Not because they care about their victims but because they seek to successfully abuse them.[3]

But this is also true of essentially moral aims. We cannot love, respect, care, advise, or feel responsible for others unless we are able to understand their roles as well. While it is true that role taking is required in order for actors to achieve their goals and it seems that while role taking action is strategic, this does not mean it is always coercive.

Another quasi-moral antecedent of successful dramaturgical interaction is something akin to moral recognition. For Goffman, a self *requires* a willing set of *deferential* others to maintain itself. Socializing with others who will recognize the self, seeking their company and interaction, is not a choice that a self has, as identity is a result of our interactions with others. Not only must the interactant be deferential, she must also be competent. Goffman notes that to be a *competent* interactant a person is taught "to be perceptive, to have feelings attached to self, and a self expressed through face, to have pride, honor, dignity, to have considerateness . . ." (Goffman, *Interaction Ritual*, 44). In *Interaction Ritual*, Goffman writes:

> The individual may desire, earn and deserve deference, but by and large he is not allowed to give it to himself, being forced to seek it from others. In seeking it from others, he finds he has added reason to seeking them out, and in turn society is given added assurance that its members will enter into interactions and relationships with one another. (58)

In addition, when playing a role we take special care to project that our identity is not consumed by the role. That is, we express a self through distancing that self from the very roles that sustain it. "Role Distance" as Goffman calls it, is making a claim that one is not "just the role" or *merely* the role in which one has been cast. Indeed, to be consumed completely by a role represents a loss of self. Role distance "is a demonstration that the role is not playing the individual but that the individual is 'playing with the role'" (Brisset and Edgley, 49).

As Goffman points out, it is often only through this process of playing with a role that an actor is able to retain her dignity. Indeed, there are times when we find those who are *not* playful within their roles to be rather disturbing or offensive. There are connections here to Sartre's notion of "bad faith." Peter Berger picks up this connection, writing, "The waiter shuffling through his appointed rounds in a cafe is in 'bad faith' insofar as he pretends to himself that the waiter role constitutes his real existence, that, if only for the hours he is hired, he *is* the waiter" (Berger, 57).

Such a conception of self and self-dignity in Goffman's writings have been referred to as "the countervailing self."[4] Selves are determined, to a large extent, by the obligations, responsibilities, and expectations attached to particular organizational roles.

> The self, then, can be seen as something that resides in the arrangements prevailing in a social system for its members. The self in this sense is not a property of the person to whom it is attributed, but dwells rather in the pattern of social control that is exerted in connection with the person himself and those around him. This special kind of institutional arrangement does not much support the self as constitute it. (Goffman, *Asylums*, 168)

However, selves respond and revolt to these institutional constraints in novel ways, and the self is *forged* through this resistance. In Goffman's words,

> The practice of reserving something of oneself from the clutch of an institution is very visible in mental hospitals and prisons but can be found in more benign and less totalistic institutions, too. I want to argue that this recalcitrance is not an incidental mechanism of defense but an essential constituent of the self. (*Asylums*, 319)

In an oft quoted passage, he writes as follows:

> Without something to belong to, we have no stable self, and yet total commitment and attachment to any social unit implies a kind of selflessness. Our sense of being a person can come from being drawn into a wider social unit; our sense of selfhood can arise through the little ways in which we resist the pull. Our status is backed by the solid buildings of the world, while our sense of personal identity often resides in the cracks. (*Asylums*, 320)

By Goffman's lights, if we carefully observe actors playing a social role, what we'll see is not a bare embracing of the role.

"We always find," he writes, "the individual employing methods to keep some distance, some elbow room, between himself and that with which others assume he should be identified" (*Asylums*, 319). Like an iron being forged in its resistance to the hardness of an anvil, a self is constructed against the strength of social roles.

> The simplest sociological view of the individual and his self is that he is to himself what his place in an organization defines him to be. When pressed, a sociologist modifies this model by granting certain complications: the self may be not yet formed or may exhibit conflicting dedications. Perhaps we should further complicate the construct by elevating these qualifications to a central place, initially defining the individual, for sociological purposes, as a stance-taking entity, a something that takes up a position somewhere between identification with an organization and opposition to it, and is ready at the slightest pressure to regain its balance by shifting its involvement in either direction. It is thus *against something* that the self can emerge. (*Asylums*, 320)

The self thus emerges, and its dignity and freedom are expressed within the ways in which those roles are toyed with and mocked—even while the role itself is embraced. In the section on role distance in *Encounters: Two Studies in the Sociology of Interaction*, Goffman delights the reader with examples of children riding a merry-go-round. In these examples Goffman illustrates that children of a certain age demonstrate to their fellows the ways in which riding the ride is not a challenge—by riding side-saddle or by riding backwards or without hands—but are still themselves challenged by the activity. The activity is taken seriously enough to be done, but not serious enough to demonstrate that the actor is taking it seriously. Watch the dance floor at a contemporary wedding, and you'll see examples of role distance. Those who dance (and perhaps they only dance at weddings) will dance, but do so while carefully expressing that they do not care about *how* they dance. This will be demonstrated with exaggerated dancing, smirks, eye rolls, and jokes. Their dancing is horrible, they know it's horrible, but it's important for them to demonstrate that they *know* this, which makes giving the impression that they don't care an important part of the activity. Thus they are able to maintain dignity, such as it is, at an indignant time. There is room for dignity in the chicken dance after all, as long as there is an opportunity to demonstrate that I am not willing to be defined by it.

For some, the roles we take on are dictated by all-encompassing institutions. These institutions, while not sharing essential features, do possess some characteristics in common. Goffman lists four. First, all aspects of life take place in the same place and are monitored by the same authority. Second, each part of a person's daily activity is conducted in the company of others. Third, the day's activities are tightly scheduled and are enforced by a system of rules set in place by the single authority. Fourth, the enforced activities are tied together into a single plan designed to fulfill the aim of the institution. Goffman provides many examples of "total institutions." These examples range from hospice care, group homes for the blind, mental hospitals, prisons, and monasteries.

We don't need to look very far today to see that institutions, such as Camp Delta at Guantanamo Bay or the temporary holding facility for detainees at Baghram Airbase, nicely fulfill the requirements for total institutions. Such institutions seem to be sandwiched between Goffman's third and fourth types of total institutions:

> A third type of total institution is organized to protect the community against what are felt to be intentional dangers to it, with the welfare of the person thus sequestered not the immediate issue: jails, penitentiaries, P.O.W. camps, and concentration camps. Fourth, there are institutions purportedly established the better to pursue some work-like task and justifying themselves only on these instrumental grounds: army barracks, ships, boarding schools, work camps, colonial compounds, and large mansions from the point of view of those who live in the servants' quarters. (*Asylums*, 5)

On the one hand, an institution like Camp Delta seems clearly designed, like a prison, to protect society from those it houses. Inmates conduct their lives and activities behind a series of symbolic walls—barbed wire, the Marine base around them, and the island of Cuba itself.[5] On the other hand, this facility also has other motives for holding these individuals: including the extraction of information.

In "total institutions" with their "all encompassing tendencies" even such attempts at playing *with* roles and the attempts at "secondary adjustments," such as practices of resistance to the institution are called, are carefully monitored, administered, and controlled. The more absolute the requirements of obedience, the more the opportunities for self-fashioning are destroyed.

Lawrence Weschler describes a similar total institution Libertad, an Uruguayan prison for political prisoners. Such an institution, it seems, was designed to deny prisoners of any ability to resist—thus robbing them of any chance at expressing dignity.

> "Day after day, rule after rule—all was a part of a grand design to make them suffer psychologically." It was precisely this drama—a prison conducted on behaviorist principles run amok—that so alarmed the visiting delegation from the International Red Cross. (131)

Weschler portrays the ways in which this total institution acted to subvert any attempt at resisting the institution. Every facet of a prisoner's life was designed for discomfort or horror. Talks with other prisoners or prison staff were taped to find places for psychological exploitation. If a prisoner complained about loud noise, the prison staff would place the prisoner next to the stairwell. If a prisoner expressed a desire to be outside, he was given a cramped, indoor job. The system of rules imposed at the prison was intentionally designed to be unintelligible. Rules changed for no reason. A rule demanding a door be open one day, demanded the next day that it remain shut. Moreover, violations met with unpredictable punishments.

> Violations were recorded with mock-scientific thoroughness, so that you were made to see that—on paper, anyway—you had indeed now committed three violations, which had such-and-such a consequence. But it was all double binds piled on more double binds. (133)

The only safe guarantee was total submission and assimilation.

In these totalizing environs, which Goffman referred to as a kind of "insanity of place," any attempt at systemic disobedience is thwarted and turned against the prisoner. The individual is unable to prepare her roles, her very "backstage" preparations are denied to her. For such an individual, there is only the self that the institution allows in the scripted expressions and the activities that the institution permits. In such a system, there can be no dignity. David Sussman's explanation of the moral wrongness of torture is very much in line with these dramaturgical observations. He writes, "We feel shame when we seem unable to keep from publicizing what we wish to keep private and hence seem unable to control the persona we present to others." (179)

MILITARY INTERROGATION

In Goffman's explorations of the ignoble, he observes that the cooperation underlying our performances and impressions (our very selves) isn't just deeply subtle (as when we play a role while at the same time playing *with* it), it's also deeply cooperational. Preventative practices are constantly performed to compensate for occurrences which may discredit a self that have not been successfully avoided—such as when accidents, slips, or gaffes occur.

Goffman refers to these as "defensive practices" when a participant employs them to save the definition of a situation, or of a self, projected by himself. When they are employed to save the definition of a situation, or of a self, projected by *another*, we call it *tact*. Goffman urges:

> Together, defensive and protective practices comprise the techniques employed to safeguard the impression fostered by an individual during his presence before others. It should be added that while we may be ready to see that no fostered impression would survive if defensive practices were not employed, we are less ready perhaps to see that few impression could survive if those who received the impression did not exert tact in their reception of it. (Goffman, *Presentation of Self*, 14)

Not only does the dramaturgical model go a long way in explaining the denial of self and dignity rendered by total institutions and the practice of torture, it also helps highlight several important lessons for the military interrogator, including highlighting some potential pitfalls, both practical and moral, military interrogators and their human intelligence sources may potentially face.

The idea of military interrogation—like the conception of torture itself—conjures many images. On one end of the spectrum one might imagine a captured soldier readily relaying tactical and strategic information to whomever might be in earshot. While on the other end of the spectrum, we might imagine a defiant prisoner of war (or some legal down-market analog) being tortured to reveal some vital information—like the location of a presumed ticking bomb or the location of his Al Qaeda collaborators. On its face, the latter scenario seems rather easily understood in categories borrowed from the stage. The interrogator and his source are the roles; there's a plot, the events of the time before the bomb is set to explode; there might be props, perhaps knives, hammers, pliers, electrodes, water tanks, barking dogs, torture warrants, and the like; and there is certainly a stage—a holding cell, a tent, a prison hallway. Each part comes with a script that's to be performed. The prisoner's role requires insolence and fear, the torturer requires contempt and coldness. As we explored at the beginning of the chapter, the spectacle of the ticking time bomb thought experiment asks us to think about what practices might be morally forbidden (and the conclusion was that there were no constraints) in extracting information from the body of a guilty brute.

But this, so far, is a bit ham handed. First, many military interrogators will explain that cases *just like* the ticking time-bomb either never have happened or, perhaps more forcefully, *could* never happen. Second, we argue, the dramaturgical categories *cannot* be applied to cases like this, nor can we consider them to be consistent with the goals of the military intelligence mission. In part, this is because the dramaturgical standpoint requires at least *two* actors, not one. (More on this in a moment.)

As one interrogator—a veteran of both Vietnam and the current conflict in Iraq—noted,

As professionals, we want to produce the most accurate and complete information possible, and we are always striving to perfect our questioning skills. Our perspective is that, beyond being morally reprehensible, torture does not satisfy the professional interrogator's need for a reliable technique that produces a verifiable truth. (Bennett, 391)

In a joint statement sent to the House Committee on the Armed Services, several former military interrogators (many of whom had experiences in several theaters of war) asserted that

> trained and experienced interrogators refute the assertion that so-called "coercive interrogation techniques" and torture are necessary to win the "War on Terror." Trained and experienced interrogators can, in fact, accomplish the intelligence gathering mission using *only* those techniques, developed and proven effective over decades, found in the Army field manual 34–52 (1992). You will also see that experienced interrogators find prisoner/detainee abuse and torture to be *counter-productive* to the intelligence gathering mission.[6]

As it turns out, those closest to the profession and art of the military interrogator will tell you that the former case, where a cooperating soldier reveals all that he knows, is closer to the actual experiences of interrogators in combat situations. "Interrogators are advised to begin with the direct approach and to continue with it unless the source refused to continue. In previous conflicts, the direct approach was found to be sufficient for about 90% of sources" (McCauley, 402). The dramaturgical model can help explain this startling fact and the corresponding perception of experienced interrogators that instead of yielding reliable information, physical and psychological abuse only suppresses it.

Of course, actionable, verifiable information—the goal of a military interrogation—will ultimately be yielded through a source's *talking*. The dramaturgical model suggests that the significance of this talk will be largely structured by the management of an impression, not the simple conveyance of information. To a trained ear, such talk can also produce important information. The interrogator's role is to build a sense of rapport, and to keep a source talking. "The key importance of the relationship with the source is evident in many of the comments made by interrogators. 'The headway we make just by acknowledging them as a human being takes us far!'" (McCauley, 402).

Indeed, as if from out of a page by Goffman himself, the new US Army Field Manual for Human Intelligence Collection states,

Regardless of the type of operation, the initial *impression* that the HUMINT [human intelligence] collector makes on the source and the approach he takes to gain the source's cooperation will have a lasting effect on the continuing relationship and the degree of success in collecting information.[7]

As interrogators themselves repeatedly state, interrogators don't target sources, they target relationships. These relationships will have the effect of creating selves, understood as dramatic personae. "The importance of the relationship between interrogator and source is particularly evident when the relationship fails. If a negative approach (fear up, ego down) does not work, it is often necessary to change interrogators" (McCauley, 405).

From the dramaturgical perspective, this is certainly to be expected. Our social roles must be plausible and consistent, because audiences demand coherence. To act as a "brute" at one moment and as a "brother" the next, would not project either of those roles, but rather would display a kind of insanity (with which no source would be willing to establish a relationship—since there would be no competent audience to engage in the cooperative project of self-construction). "The source *wants* to talk," remarked one interrogator, "it's my job to become the person he wants to talk to."[8]

Successful interrogations aim at *cultivating* relationships and social empathy. The consequence of these relationships (and this even includes antagonistic relationships) is that selves are fashioned, maintained, and urged to stability. It's *only* these sorts of selves that will be capable of supplying verifiable, reliable, actionable intelligence through the drama that their stories tell.

But establishing rapport is an art which requires the moral requisites teased out of Goffman's analysis. The interrogator must be competent, deferential, and perhaps above all, have tact.

The catch is that non-abusive techniques require linguistic expertise, cultural sensitivity, situational awareness, flexible thinking, self-mastery, and capacity to empathize with foreigners and enemies. These skills—the product of high aptitude, much training, and long mentorship—contrast with the ignorance, bigotry, and lack of emotional control that can accompany . . . abusive techniques. (Arrigo and Wagner, 396).

Interrogators must also have in their repertoire the ability to perform many roles. Indeed, the interrogation field manual calls for this. It lists brief descriptions of 18 "approaches" which often read like scripts from a play that are meant to help an interrogator develop rapport. Each approach fosters a different kind of relationship and thus each allows the source to maintain or express a different kind of identity.

The interrogator must be fluid and flexible when it comes to his approaches and his own role. From the dramaturgical perspective, this means first that the interrogator's needs include an enormous role distance *with* the role of interrogator. Should the interrogator overly embrace the role *of* the interrogator (i.e. should the interrogator overly identify *with* the role), he faces potential moral problems. As social psychologists have noted,

> [T]he interrogator's skills can have a downside. The interior cost of pretending but withholding empathy can be considerable. It is possible to lose the feeling of authenticity in feeling and expressing empathy in relationships outside of work. Should an interrogator turn his skills toward improving what can be gotten from colleagues, friends, spouses, or children? All interrogators feel this tension; each draws his or her own line to separate life and work. Some interrogators cannot turn off the analysis stage and can only commit to not using the emotional openings that come their way from friends and family. (McCauley, 408)

The interrogator must also have enormous flexibility and role distance in order to manage the role *conflicts* which come with his work. In addition to mastering the several "approaches" listed in the field manual, the interrogator also must disentangle the empathy with a source that comes with many of the interrogator's "approaches" with the role of promoting the best interests of the military he serves.

Lastly, an interrogator must have flexibility *within* the role of interrogator. Should an interrogator overly identify with one of the approaches—like "fear up"—there may be violent consequences. This warning is particularly salient given that the sort of self promoted by the military—itself a "total institution"—is one of role rigidity. Roles are not to be challenged or toyed with, but instead whole-heartedly adopted. "Successful interrogators [on the other hand] tend to be open-minded, tolerant, imaginative, curious, and unregimented. These qualities are at odds with traditional military doctrine, discipline, and criteria for promotion" (Arrigo and Bennet, 416).

Indeed the war overseas has seen just this sort of identification. Many experienced interrogators have been horrified by the addition and wide proliferation of the new, though unofficial, approach known as "monstering" by what they perceive as amateurs denigrating their profession. This particular warning is the flip-side of the observation made by Nietzsche in *Human, All Too Human.*

> The profession of almost every man, even the artist, begins with hypocrisy, as he imitates from the outside, copies what is effective. The man who always wears the mask of a friendly countenance eventually has to gain power over benevolent moods without which the expression of friendliness cannot be forced—and eventually then these moods gain power over him, and he *is* benevolent. (51)

In closing this section, we return to the example of torture—the far end of the spectrum of military interrogation. The dramaturgical model also reveals, we think, much about why torture is counterproductive. It's not just because anyone will say anything to relieve the burden of pain (which, of course, might be true too), but rather because understood through the dramaturgical lens, the victim is *no longer a self*. The techniques of torture, not just the overtly physical but also the psychological, including humiliation, isolation, starvation, and the like, serve to dismantle a self—not transform a self into an actor willing to play and create his part.

What we think the dramaturgical model suggests—perhaps most dramatically—is that our intuitions about emergency cases like the ticking-time-bomb case are horribly misinformed. That thought experiment presupposes that the abuse of a source will in fact generate the required information. Instead, the dramaturgical model supposes (and the experience of military interrogators corroborates) that the truth of the matter is, in fact, quite the opposite. The more an interrogator is able to build rapport, to use his mastery of tact to allow a source to express an image of the self, the more likely it is that in this expressive talk, verifiable and previously unknown information will be uncovered. As two social psychologists familiar with the profession of the military interrogator recently wrote, "In a high-stakes, bad-bet situation of this sort [involved in a ticking bomb], they would resort to their best, deeply relational interrogation techniques, not squander the fragile opportunity through torture" (Arrigo and Wagner, 396).

What has been investigated in this chapter, and more specifically the way it has been explored, should be considered as tentative and exploratory. Using the language of the stage to gaze at the institutions that permit torture and the selves that are victimized by it, dramaturgical analysis reveals that there are hidden horrors located at the site of real torture. The practice of torture requires, at a minimum, two actors—and, as a result of the practice, each actor suffers a loss of self. The victim of course, through her mistreatment and inhabitation in a total institution, a place of insanity, loses the option to resist an administered identity and her tormenter's heteronymous will. Her jailors, for their part, also lose out. To mistreat a prisoner, to assault the defenseless in the name of an ideal, a party, or a country is to overly embrace the role. To be the brute—to abuse without flinching, without comfort or charity—one must lose oneself completely in one's macabre tasks. This, too, represents a loss of self and a closed opportunity for the expression of dignity.

Goffman himself would perhaps want to stress that this framework for thinking about torture is, indeed, just one of many. Goffman writes at the conclusion of *The Presentation of Everyday Life*,

The claim that all the world's a stage is sufficiently commonplace for readers to be familiar with its limitations and tolerant of its presentations, knowing that at any time they will easily be able to demonstrate to themselves that it is not to be taken too seriously. (254)

He continues a few sentences further, "Scaffolds, after all, are to build other things with, and should be erected with an eye to taking them down" (254).

This philosophical inroad into sociology and social psychology has been less a sustained sociological or philosophical treatise than it has been an invitation to think beyond the borders of our discipline. Lastly, what we hope, at the very least, to have made plausible with this incursion is that those who find themselves arguing in favor of torture's permissibility also seem to be suffering from another illusion about the nature of interrogational torture: that it is ever effective. This analysis has thus tried to illuminate and explain in dramatic terms what one particular kind of applied social psychologist—the experienced military interrogator—has known all along. Torture is counter to the goals of military intelligence and its institutional practice is anathema to those social girders which support the formation of a self with the substance and dignity worthy of our veneration. "Many gods have been done away with, but the individual himself stubbornly remains as a deity of considerable importance" (Goffman, *Interaction Ritual*, 95).

CHAPTER FIVE

THE COMMUNICATIVE MODEL OF TORTURE

UNDERSTANDING INSTITUTIONALLY PERMISSIVE TORTURE

INTRODUCTORY REMARKS

The stubborn endurance of torture as a practice, and thus as an ethical and political issue, has been recently demonstrated in the United States' "War on Terror." Attempts at understanding the practice and explaining why it occurs have typically focused on psychological explanations which include such categories as indoctrination, sadism, and susceptibility to authority. However, placing perpetrators at the center of the explanation provides an incomplete account of the practice.

Psychological categories, while helpful in understanding the behavior of perpetrators, are by themselves incomplete. If the purpose of understanding torture is to eradicate it, then a more robust account of torture is required. In particular, an account of the practice ought to include an account of the structure of the institutions which, either explicitly or implicitly, permit torture. It is an examination of this structure that is the focus of our attention in the current chapter.

The model of communicative action developed by Jürgen Habermas yields valuable insights for understanding the institutions which allow torture and the agents who engage in it. Arguably, the very purpose of the sort of torture recently on display in the American media is the forceful establishment of distorted communication. The institutions which permit torture are, in fact, particularly vulnerable to committing this perversion of the "performative attitude," which is a paradigm case of latently strategic action involving subterfuge, deception, and above all, power. These Habermasian-inspired insights provide not only an institutional diagnosis of the problems which led to the mistreatment of detainees at the Bagram Air Base, despite the efforts of those in command to prevent such abuse, but they also suggest an institutional corrective.

INSTITUTIONALLY PERMISSIVE TORTURE: SOME PRELIMINARIES

Even as the young Afghan man was dying before them, his American jailors continued to torment him.

The prisoner, a slight, 22-year-old taxi driver known only as Dilawar, was hauled from his cell at the detention center in Bagram, Afghanistan, at around 2 a.m. to answer questions about a rocket attack on an American base. When he arrived in the interrogation room, an interpreter who was present said, his legs were bouncing uncontrollably in the plastic chair and his hands were numb. He had been chained by the wrists to the top of his cell for much of the previous four days.

Mr Dilawar asked for a drink of water, and one of the two interrogators, Specialist Joshua R. Claus, 21, picked up a large plastic bottle. But first he punched a hole in the bottom, the interpreter said, so as the prisoner fumbled weakly with the cap, the water poured out over his orange prison scrubs. The soldier then grabbed the bottle back and began squirting the water forcefully into Mr Dilawar's face.

"Come on, drink!" the interpreter said Specialist Claus had shouted, as the prisoner gagged on the spray. "Drink!"

At the interrogators' behest, a guard tried to force the young man to his knees. But his legs, which had been pummeled by guards for several days, could no longer bend. An interrogator told Mr Dilawar that he could see a doctor after they finished with him. When he was finally sent back to his cell, though, the guards were instructed only to chain the prisoner back to the ceiling.

"Leave him up," one of the guards quoted Specialist Claus as saying.

Several hours passed before an emergency room doctor finally saw Mr Dilawar. By then he was dead, his body beginning to stiffen. It would be many months before Army investigators learned a final horrific detail: Most of the interrogators had believed Mr Dilawar was an innocent man who simply drove his taxi past the American base at the wrong time.[1] (*The New York Times*, May 20, 2005)

What happened to Mr Dilawar was, as is known now, part of a larger pattern of abuse committed at Bagram and elsewhere—at least eight detainees are documented as dying in US custody in Afghanistan. To say that the violence done to Mr Dilawar and the others was wrong is as philosophically obvious as anything we are likely to run across. Nevertheless, such abuse did occur, and it was committed by an institution that not only had an explicit interest in, and commitment to, preventing this abuse; but it also *actively* and *overtly* sought to *prevent* abuse of this kind. The fact that the above event happened is indeed tragic—that it was perpetrated by those trained to worry about the articles of the Geneva Convention and the Uniform Code of Military Justice is downright bewildering.

Let us begin with an assumption that we won't argue for here: the sort of violence in the above case is inherently institutional. We take this to be a rather minimal claim. While those individuals who perpetrated those deeds which led to Dilawar's death are certainly the primary bearers of moral culpability, the institution, including its command structures, its objectives, its methods of reaching those objectives, the training of its workers, indeed even its culture, are also morally implicated in the death of Mr Dilawar. That is, the final *moral* explanation of Dilawar's death, whatever that looks like, won't only include facts about those who committed the fatal blows. It is for this reason that we refer to this sort of violence as *institutional* violence. (This is taken in contrast to other situations of violence, such as mob violence, where there are multiple assailants, but where there is not an institutional structure which plays a role in the moral explanation of the assault.)

A framework for understanding moral actions, if it is not to be of conceptual interest alone, ought to satisfy two conditions. First, the framework should provide an overall method of *describing* the act (thus, in a sense the framework would turn a behavior or set of behaviors into a moral action). The framework should yield an *explanation* of the sort of moral act or event in question in terms of the experiences of those committing it. And it should also reveal morally salient features of the experiences of those who are victims of the act or event. This first condition is an *explanatory* condition—it answers a *why* question (why is that action a moral one, and why did it happen?). Second, the framework should address the issues of both deterrence and redress. That is, it ought to suggest ways in which the action or event under consideration can be prevented in the future. Furthermore, it should also provide, from the perspective of the victim, ways in which the action can be restituted or repaired. This second condition answers a *what now* question (now that we better understand the action, how should we proceed?). Thus, whatever framework we ultimately chose for thinking about torture in cases like the one above, that framework should have both *diagnostic* and *prescriptive* potential. So we should judge the value of the framework through its contribution to the description and explanation of the act, and we should judge it for what it recommends as a deterrent and remedy.[2]

The reader will recall that we developed a robust taxonomy of types of torture in Chapter One. Our focus, as we pointed out there, is on *interrogational* torture, though what we have so far said about interrogational torture has broad implications for *every* type of torture. Having explored the economic model and the phenomenological model in some detail, we will turn our attention in this chapter to the *communicative model*. Before doing so, however, it will be worthwhile to reiterate a previous point: we do not think these models need be mutually exclusive—with each other or of any of the other rival models. We can treat them as "analytical frameworks" for observing different *moral aspects* of the same event.

INSTITUTIONALLY PERMISSIVE TORTURE: THE COMMUNICATIVE MODEL

The communicative model takes Habermas's system of communicative action as a template. Sometimes the Habermasian vocabulary will apply rather directly to the exploration, while at other times, perhaps, the application will seem more metaphorical—though in both cases the vocabulary will helpfully illuminate the practice.

Indeed, the interrogation which led to Dilawar's death took place in a larger context of a war on terror involving the US military (and others). Indeed, as the military is often called a microcosm of society itself, it is a ripe target for the tools of a critical theory of society (which is what Habermas's system is, of course, designed for). What we want to exploit, for the purpose of showing the ways in which Habermas's model can be useful, are several symmetries between Habermas's model and certain procedural patterns which led to systematic abuse at Bagram, and ultimately culminated in Dilawar's death.

Habermas's system of the theory of communicative action furnishes the communicative model of interrogational torture with many helpful categories. For the sake of space, we'll focus on just a few here. (Also, we'll take the antecedent plausibility of these distinctions for granted. Our aim is not to *justify* them as aspects of a well-grounded critical theory; we merely want to explore how useful they are in helping us think about interrogational torture.) These categories are the performative attitude (this includes Habermas's distinction between communicative action and latently strategic action), the concept of systematically distorted communication, and corresponding notions of the lifeworld and the colonization of the lifeworld (including the social and personal pathologies that such colonization generates in the structures of the lifeworld).

We want to focus first rather narrowly by looking at the event of interrogation itself. The goal of the interrogation, ostensibly, is truth. In the case of the Bagram collection point, interrogatees were typically picked up in Special Operations raids in various parts of Afghanistan and in the northern territories of Pakistan. These individuals were shipped *en masse* to several different detention and processing centers around Afghanistan (including Kabul, Kandahar, and secret CIA safe houses). At Bagram, US Army interrogators would find themselves confronted with a variety of detainees. Some were Al Qaeda members, some were their Taliban hosts, some were minor criminals or malcontents sold to the United States by rival tribes because of grudges or rivalries, and others still were innocent civilians (they were simply in the wrong place at the wrong time). The task immediately assigned to these interrogators (dispatched for year-long missions) was to sort out, exactly, who was who. Once they felt that they were reasonably sure that they had identified prisoners of interest (say, who had knowledge of Al Qaeda or Taliban activities, and especially those who had some sort of tie to western Europe), these prisoners were screened out for further interrogation.

Interrogators wanted to know from *these* prisoners about their routes into Afghanistan, who hosted them, where they stayed, what sorts of weapons they saw, who else traveled with them, what their purpose was, how they were funded, and the like. Those prisoners who were deemed especially important were then sent on to Cuba (presumably for further interrogation)— or, as we've learned, to other countries in a process known as "extraordinary rendition."

On the surface, interrogations are carried out just like any other conversation. And, indeed Habermas provides us with a helpful way to think about these conversations. His model demarcates three different kinds of speech acts that a speaker may perform (which correspond to the three different ways in which a speaker may be challenged—and any utterance may be challenged in any of these ways). However, only two sorts of claims, claims to truth and claims to rightness (theoretical and normative claims, respectively) are *discursively* redeemable. To say that these types of speech acts can be redeemed discursively means that speakers can offer *evidence* as to why what they are claiming theoretically is true, and they can offer *reasons* as to why what they are claiming normatively is analogously true. The defense of any challenge to these claims will come in the form of reasons (which themselves, of course, can be challenged).

However, there is one sort of way in which our utterances may be challenged that is *not* discursively redeemable. This is the truthfulness (or sincerity) of what we say. Again, the truthfulness of my expression can always be doubted and challenged— but these doubts, on Habermas's model, *cannot* be allayed or dismissed discursively. Furthermore, by Habermas's lights, speaking with the intent to reach mutual understanding or consensus (which Habermas refers to as the fundamental *telos* of speech) is the *primary* kind of language use. Speaking with strategic intent (where the intention is not to come to a mutual consensus, but rather to influence or *manipulate* the hearer) is a *parasitic* mode of speech. When actors engage each other with the intent of reaching an understanding, they are adopting what he calls the "performative attitude."[3]

In interrogations, as in genuine conversation, all of these validity claims are on display. However, unlike normal conversation, the goal of the conversation in an interrogation, from the point of view of *both* participants, is obvious (especially in the situation that detainees and interrogators found themselves in at

Bagram). For the interrogator, the point is to assess the intelligence value of his interlocutor. For the detainee, the point is providing information that would lead to his release.

Typically, in the case of Bagram, interrogators would see two patterns. First, if the detainee was Afghani, they would explain that they were a civilian that hates the Taliban and did not partake in any fighting (if they did, it was under severe duress). If the detainee was foreign (from Western Europe in particular), they indicated that they went to Pakistan or Afghanistan in search of a simpler life and an Islamic bride. They had no ties to Al Qaeda and did not participate in any fighting. For some detainees, the story told was truthful and sincere, for others it was not. It was, indeed, just the task of the interrogator to discern the sincere from the insincere. Thinking again about Habermasian pragmatics, *because* of the fact that the truthfulness of speech acts *cannot* be redeemed discursively (by simply exchanging reasons), the interrogators had a very difficult and exasperating job. (Their preferred method of detecting insincerity was through *indirect* discursive means by looking for inconsistencies in and between detainees' stories.)

Indeed, the majority of training *as* an interrogator is to learn how to assess sincerity, and also how to leverage it by manipulation.[4] Taking for granted that reaching an understanding and adopting the performative attitude is the *fundamental* use of language, one might expect two consequences for the means for carrying out interrogation. The first is that simply asking a detainee for the desired information would be most productive. Indeed, according to the Army training manual, this turns out to be the case. This method is known as the "Direct Approach." Chris Mackey, an interrogator who worked at Bagram notes

> in our schoolhouse training, if we didn't ask a pertinent question first (before trying to orchestrate an approach), we were immediately knocked down on our evaluations. The direct approach, we were told, would work on more than 95 percent of all POWs . . . (Mackey and Miller, 479)

Second, taking for granted that the goal of reaching an understanding is the *natural* mode of language use and provided the failure of the "Direct Approach," we would also expect that one way to achieve interrogational success is by trying to catch detainees off guard. That is, to try to *reset* them to their "natural" performative attitude. Mackey describes anecdotal evidence of just such a sense of the "naturalness" of speaking with communicative intent even when one is *strongly* motivated to deceive. He recalls the following of one of his first interrogation sessions, with a man known as "Prisoner 140":

> For hours this nonsense continued. Prisoner 140 claimed he couldn't remember the name of the hotel, the names of friends in his native Algeria, the name of his landlady in Hamburg, or even the name of his Imam at the mosque. It was incredible, and it was infuriating . . . When prisoners were questioned, everyone's name had been "lost" to fragile memory. There were no identifying features, no addresses, no telephone numbers. In the recesses of our minds where logic ruled, we knew it was impossible for so many prisoners to have forgotten so much. But we were confounded by the utter directness of the lies. It wasn't a kind of cocktail party fib, easily seen through, easily peeled away. It was the mindless refutation of the obvious. . . .
>
> The story [given by Prisoner 140] was nearly identical to every other prisoner's . . . Against my instinct, I began almost to want the man's tale to be true. It would be easier if it were.
>
> An hour later, I noticed I was no longer squinting at my notebook. A ray of light from the morning's sunrise had found the open seam in the tent. I had spent more than six hours with 140. We were both fatigued and frozen. The night had been a waste . . . As I gathered my belongings, I noticed . . . a reminder to ask 140 who had owned the house where he'd stayed in Jalalabad.
>
> The prisoner had already stood up from the metal chair, had had his cap pulled down over his eyes by the MP, and was being led away. I stepped around the table, pulled up the rim of the prisoner's cap, and asked, "Who owns the house in Jalalabad?"
>
> Without any hesitation, Prisoner 140 replied, "Al-Jezari."
>
> Then 140 raised his head with a jerk that might have been caused by an electric shock. The prisoner had yielded a name. He had slipped. (Mackey and Miller, 11–13)

Another way in which Habermas's model helps us think about interrogation and its tendency to decline into violence is through the concept of "systematically distorted communication." Distorted communication is "communication that becomes so restricted that it is no longer cognitively reliable" and when it "is no longer the intersubjective medium by which agents could reflect upon how they use their rational capacities" (Bohman, 3). Distorted communication is "systematic" in the sense that it is communication which, in its attempt, violates the normative conditions which make mutual understanding through communication possible.[5]

For Habermas, what confers a speech act with its meaning are its "acceptability conditions." That is, we understand a speech act when we know what sorts of reasons a speaker could use to defend it. What type of reason that would be used primarily to defend the claim is what, in the end, makes it the *kind of claim* that it is (a constative, regulative, or expressive claim). For language use to count as reaching a consensus, it must be backed by the warranty of exchanging reasons through discourse, should communication become problematic. Speakers and hearers can, in principle, always demand explicit justification in second-order communication (or "discourse") in order to reach an understanding. Because the meaning of our utterances is thus tied to practices of argumentation, the acceptance of such a claim provides the utterance with its intersubjective "binding and bonding force."

Moreover, in order to count as "reaching understanding," the argumentative practices must exhibit four features. First, each participant must have an equal chance to initiate and continue communication. Second, each participant must have an equal chance to make assertions, recommendations, and explanations, and to challenge justifications. These are sometimes referred to as "symmetry conditions."[6] Third, all must have an equal chance to express their wishes, feelings, and intentions. Finally, speakers must act in contexts of action as if "there is an equal distribution of chances to order and resist orders, to promise and to refuse, to be accountable for one's conduct and to demand accountability from others" (Benhabib, 285). These last two conditions are sometimes called the "reciprocity condition," and refer "to existing action contexts, and requires a suspension of situations of untruthfulness and duplicity on the one hand, and of inequality and subordination on the other" (Benhabib, 285). In order to count as having reached a consensus, the argumentative process must involve a norm of *freedom*, since to be convinced an interlocutor must be persuaded through the use of her own free will. The reasons I offer must become reasons for her. In addition, the process of argumentation must demonstrate a norm of *justice* in the form of the "reciprocal and symmetrical distribution of rights among participants" (Benhabib, 286).

As we've seen, the interrogator's task is to assess the truthfulness of the detainee, but this is difficult because the interrogator knows that the detainee has a motivation for insincerely portraying himself in a certain way. Reciprocally, the detainee knows that the interrogator's purpose in conversation is to yield as much useful information as possible and that the interrogator will use subterfuge and manipulation to do so. Because both detainee and interrogator are aware of these facts, we can think about this setting as "systematically distorted" at the level of sincerity, which (again) is a norm implicit in any successful communicative utterance.[7]

If we accept this account of "systematic distortion," we might *a priori* expect that it will have consequences for both the interrogatee *and* interrogator (for the interrogator it will lead to lifeworld pathologies which will then manifest into physical abuse for the interrogatee). As an interrogator's attempts at trying to ascertain truthfulness are systematically undermined by the very process of ascertaining truthfulness, it would not be far-fetched to imagine that a frustrated interrogator would transition from attempting to *manipulate* a detainee for the purpose of establishing truthfulness (through deceit and duplicity—that is, through his own use of insincerity), to the actual *physical* coercion of a detainee (persuasion with the use of reason, when thwarted, becomes persuasion with the use of force).

Moreoever, Habermas's model reveals that there may be another reason why such systematically distorted conversational encounters might lead to violence. For an interrogator, the interogatee represents not only a human being, but also an opportunity. Indeed the very *point* of the conversation, what brings these two individuals together, is the extraction of information. Their relationship is structurally designed to be strategic, *not* communicative. For the interrogator, the detainee is a tool used for the purposes of gathering information—perhaps not unlike a thermometer or telescope. The more an interrogator encounters resistance from a source, the more that interrogator must treat the detainee strategically and not communicatively—that is, as an equal provider of reasons in a symmetrical and reciprocal relationship. Habermas's model would thus suggest that the more resistance a detainee provides, the more *de-humanized* he will become to the interrogator.

Indeed, just such a tendency slide into coercion was documented by Dr Michael Gelles, the chief psychologist at the Naval Criminal Investigation Service. Dr Gelles warned his superiors of (what he called) a "force drift": a natural inclination "to uncontrolled abuse when interrogators encounter resistance."[8] He further warned that, "once the initial barrier against the use of force had been breached, . . . 'force drift' would almost certainly begin . . . [and] if left unchecked, force levels, [including] torture, could be reached."[9]

Not only does the communicative model borrowed from Habermas philosophically illuminate this psychological tendency, it can also help us understand the very methods that interrogators used, when so frustrated, to punish and coerce their charges.[10] The procedures that interrogators used to punish their charges, commonly referred to as "stress and duress" techniques (which include sitting or kneeling in painful positions for long periods of time, and standing with arms extended until told to stop), when looked at through the lens of Habermas's model, had a rather insidious nature. While the interrogator's efforts are disrupted (and so their frustrations are located) at the level of *sincerity*—which refers to the detainee's subjective world—the interrogators themselves then punished detainees at the site of the detainees' *subjectivity*, creating a sort of communicatively distorted phenomenology. As the CIA's *Kubark Manual on Counter-Intelligence* maintains: "It has been plausibly suggested that, whereas pain inflicted on a person from the outside may actually focus or intensify his will to resist, his resistance is likelier to be sapped by pain which he *seems* to inflict upon himself."[11] As Alfred McCoy, a historian of recent torture, notes,

once the subject is disoriented, interrogators can then move on to the stage of self-inflicted pain through techniques such as enforced standing with arms extended [as witnessed at Bagram]. In this latter phase, victims are made *to feel responsible for their own suffering*, thus inducing them to alleviate their agony by capitulating to the power of their interrogators. (52)

Through these techniques, the source of the pain *communicated* to the detainees itself is distorted. Moreover, when interrogators issue veiled threats of either "stress and duress" techniques, or of something more serious, as the CIA *Human Resource Exploitation Training Manual* explains, it should always be implied that the subject himself is to blame by using words such as, "You leave me no other choice but to . . . " He should never be told to "comply or else."[12] So such methods of punishing detainees, Habermas's model suggests, are retributive in nature. While the interrogator suffers a communicative frustration from the detainee, so the punishments of the interrogator frustrate the communication that the detainee will have with his own body.

While the interrogation's distorted communication can have appalling mental and physical consequences for the interrogatees, Habermas's system of communicative action implies that such distorted communication will take a broader toll. As we've seen, Habermas's position on the performative attitude includes propositional attitudes to three "worlds": The objective, the intersubjective, and the subjective. The process that allows speakers to differentiate reference to three different worlds takes place against the background of what Habermas calls the "lifeworld." For Habermas, the lifeworld is an essential place of rationalization. The lifeworld is the "'horizon' within which human beings refer to items in the objective, subjective and normative worlds" (Outhwaite, 86). As Habermas puts it further,

> Under the functional aspect of mutual understanding, communicative action serves to transmit and renew cultural knowledge; under the aspect of coordinating action, it serves social integration and the establishment of solidarity; finally, under the aspect of socialization, communicative action serves the formation of personal identities. The symbolic structures of the lifeworld are reproduced by way of the continuation of valid knowledge, stabilization of group solidarity,

and socialization of responsible actors. . . . Corresponding to these processes of cultural reproduction, social integration and socialization are the structural components of the life-world: culture, society, person. (137)

A lifeworld free from distorted communication is the site of the formation of *rational* cultures, societies, and persons. When the path to communicative action is blocked or disrupted, when consensus formation is not a part of these aspects within the lifeworld, crises can erupt within these spheres.

The corresponding failures take the form of loss of meaning, crises of legitimation and orientation, in the case of *cultural reproduction*, anomie and the absence of social solidarity in the case of *social integration*, and psychopathologies (especially those of the ego) in the case of *socialization*. (Outhwaite, 87, our emphasis)

Interrogators at Bagram would sometimes spend up to 24 hours in a day trying to assess sincerity claims through manipulation and duplicity. While we've seen that such protracted exposure to distorted communication can lead to abuse by the creation of conditions of a *distorted subjective experience* through "stress and duress" techniques, given Habermas's claim that lifeworld socialization and reproduction ought to be done under rational, distortion-free contexts of communication, we might expect such a length of time in conditions of distorted communication to also harm the interrogator. More specifically, we would expect to find in the interrogator, as Habermas's system would have it suffering crises at the site of socialization and social integration which would exhibit as predicaments of motivation, alienation, or other psychopathologies. And indeed, Chris Mackey, one of the interrogators in charge at Bagram describes a fellow interro-gator who seems to manifest *all* of the above. He recounts as follows:

I knew Fitzgerald was serious . . . but thought I might be able to short-circuit his gloom. . . . I could tell from the way his arms were hanging down between his legs in a kind of tired cowboy posture. He was tired in a sense that was more profound than the rest of the unit, deeper even than the dark circles under his eyes would lead someone to guess. . . . "I really hate this place. I hate the people, I hate the prisoners, I hate the . . . army, and I hate *you* . . . This place is insane, Mackey. I'm telling you, it's insane . . . Nobody has any . . . idea what we're doing, and everybody figures the only answer is to redouble our efforts. I can't even begin to think about doing this . . . until October. Look at the Bureau guys. Look at the [CIA]. Those jokers go home every few weeks. Somebody, somewhere in those organizations knows you can't just throw interrogators into this thing day after day without a break, exposing them to this G.I. Joe versus Cobra crap day in and day out and expect them to keep on truckin." (231)

While at this point, we have only discussed the ways in which lifeworld colonization, in the form of systematically distorted communication can create crises of lifeworld socialization which, in turn, can negatively affect both detainee and interrogator, there are indeed other ways in which the crises of lifeworld colonization can, indirectly, lead to detainee violence. The military itself, with its rigid chain of command, actively fosters asymmetrical communication punctuated by the transmission of power. While such asymmetrical conditions are probably most efficient for the organization's overall militaristic needs, it surely also leads to the sort of lifeworld crises mentioned by Habermas.

There are two additional sites of lifeworld crises worth mentioning here. They concern the lifeworld components of cultural reproduction and social integration. Cultural integration is responsible for "valid knowledge," and it requires processes where knowledge claims can always be checked and questioned through symmetrical communication procedures and argumentative practices. The interrogators at Bagram, however, had no control over their mission, interrogational procedure, or the fate of their detainees. For these interrogators and their superiors, this system of asymmetrical communication procedures led to a crisis of legitimation such that the legitimizing and validation of knowledge that the interrogators produced became problematic *simply because of the fact that it was produced at all.* Chris Mackey notes one instance where he and his fellow interrogators were told by their command "to produce comprehensive reports

on every prisoner in custody, each concluding with a recommendation that the prisoner be detained (by the Afghan government), shipped off to GTMO, or repatriated" (231). This new
policy decision, which left no room for interrogators to discuss
or defend their findings with their superiors, led to a paradoxical
result. Mackey remarks as follows:

> Trying to take advantage of this recanvassing to glean more
> intelligence, the interrogators started spreading word that
> Cuba was filling up and that those deemed untruthful would
> get turned over to the Afghans. It worked, and the unit started
> getting pats on the back from the [immediate] command for
> the new information being collected. But the command in
> Kuwait was less impressed. To the senior officers at Camp
> Doha, the new reports just meant the interrogators were
> catching their earlier mistakes. As a result, some prisoners of
> dubious intelligence value were shipped to GTMO *largely
> because no one at Doha trusted the reports recommending they
> be released.* (222, emphasis ours)

There are also reasons to think that there were other lifeworld
crises, such as a loss of meaning. Due to bureaucratic–political
systems over which the interrogators had no control, the word
"torture" became a term emptied of substance. Alfred McCoy
notes that during this period "the White House was quietly
rescinding legal constraints on brutal interrogation, and may
well have contributed to a climate conducive to covert, yet offi-
cially sanctioned, torture" (112). Moreover, in late 2001 and
throughout 2002 the Justice Department gave the CIA a narrow
interpretation of the UN antitorture convention and they argued
that the Geneva Conventions and the US War Crimes Act did
not apply to the Afghanistan conflict. At this time Assistant
Attorney General Bybee recommended to the White House legal
counsel that "To constitute torture under U.S. statute, the physical pain must, he said, 'be equivalent in intensity to the pain
accompanying serious physical injury, such as organ failure,
impairment of bodily function, or even death'"[13] (317). Central to
this new interpretation was an emphasis on the intention of
the interrogator. Thus any interrogator who tortured but later
claimed that his aim was to gain information rather than inflict

pain was not guilty of torture. This new interpretation of "torture" removes so much moral substance from the term that Tindale's categories of "interrogational torture" and "deterrent torture" would be rendered self-contradictory. Only the category of "dehumanizing torture" would remain. Not only did this "loss of meaning" suffered by the moral category of torture conflict with antecedent ways of thinking about it, it also explicitly conflicted with the training and indoctrination of interrogators like Mackey.[14] Such an emptying of this moral category trickled down the ranks, finally ending up with the interrogators themselves. As a result, Bagram saw in each successive generation of replacing interrogational unit an increased kind of "anomie" surfacing—if we take that to mean a lack of law or ethical standard. The Geneva Conventions were interpreted less and less broadly, and thus their power to guide interrogations was weakened.

At this point, we've only explored ways in which turning to Habermas's model of communicative action can help illuminate the *why* question of the success conditions of moral frameworks. What we've suggested above is that Habermas's model provides us with a way to see the abuses at Bagram (what we called institutionally permissive torture) as systematically induced lifeworld pathologies which were simultaneously fostered through systematically distorted communication.

We have not yet addressed how Habermas's model can help answer the *what now* question, but from what the model has already illustrated there are some possibilities. One recommendation that the model might make is that any remedy needs to counteract the distorted communication produced in the interrogational setting. One suggestion, as mentioned by the interrogator above, is not only to reduce the amount of overall time interrogators spend assessing the sincerity of detainees and, in addition, to increase the time they spend with individuals outside their own unit of interrogators. If Habermas's model is right, this will have the consequence of reducing the lifeworld crises that can manifest themselves as "force drift," and because of this it might alleviate one of the root causes of the abuse.

Another suggestion, which comes from both Habermas's model, and from experience, might be to change the very methods of interrogation. Marine Major Sherwood F. Moran was a legendary interrogator in a conflict very similar to the one that the United States (and her allies) face in the war on terror: a determined, relentless enemy from an "alien and hostile culture" coupled with the need to produce quick and reliable intelligence. Major Moran was an interrogator in the Second World War; his specialty was gathering intelligence from captured Japanese prisoners. He was "among the most effective interrogators in ·the Pacific Island campaigns of 1944 and 1945," supplying complete Japanese order-of-battle intelligence on Saipan and Tinian "within forty-eight hours of landing."

Moran wrote a sort of training manual to his fellow interrogators, and it has since become a sort of classic. "The Marine Corps Interrogator Translator Teams Association (MCITTA), a group of active-duty and retired Marine intelligence personnel, calls Moran's report one of the 'timeless documents' in the field and says it has long been 'a standard read' for insiders" (Budiansky, 32). Dr James Corum, a professor at the U.S. Army Command and General Staff College, says that "Moran's philosophy has repeatedly been affirmed in subsequent wars large and small. 'Know their language, know their culture, and treat the captured enemy as a human being'" (Budiansky, 32).

In his report, Moran writes that

> I often tell a prisoner right at the start what my attitude is! I consider a prisoner (i.e. a man who has been captured and disarmed and in a perfectly *safe* place) as out of the war, out of the picture, and thus, in a way, not an enemy . . . Then forget, as it were, the "enemy" stuff, and the "prisoner" stuff. I tell them to forget it, telling them I am *talking as a human being to a human being*. (Budiansky, 33)

"Every soldier," Moran observed, has a "story" he desperately *wants* to tell. The interrogator's job is to provide the atmosphere that allows the prisoner to tell it. Moran wrote that "the first and most important victory" is getting "into the mind and into the heart" of the prisoner and achieving an "intellectual and spiritual" rapport with him.[15] Moran further observes that to gather useful information, an interrogator, who Moran wishes to think of instead as an "interviewer" must have dignity and a proper sense of values, but withal friendly, open, and frank. Moreover, he recommends that,

> One must be absolutely sincere. I mean that one must not just assume the above attitudes in order to gain the prisoner's confidence and get him to talk. He will know the difference. You must get him to know by the expression on your face, the glance of your eye, the tone of your voice, that you do think that "the men of the four seas are brothers," to quote a Japanese (and Chinese) proverb. (Moran, 250)

In concluding, what we've explored here are ways in which Habermas's model of communicative action can have concrete applicability to cases of institutional violence—where human beings, in the context of broader strategic goals, abuse other human beings in the open and with impunity. What we've offered here are *preliminary* suggestions for ways in which the theory of communicative action can provide a framework for describing this violence (in this case as lifeworld crises on the level of person, society, and culture) and for *explaining* why such violence took place (because of prolonged exposure to systematically distorted communication which itself took place in broader contexts of asymmetrical power and communication procedures). This model also offers us the moral reminder that should we wish to reduce violence of this sort and thus increase the chance that *justice* and *freedom* will flourish, our institutions (military or otherwise) ought to be developed with just those moral categories as an engineering principle—and Habermas's model provides us with a method of doing just that.

CHAPTER SIX

ASSESSING THE VARIETIES OF TORTURE

CONCLUDING REFLECTIONS ON A RECURRENT PROBLEM

Torture does not seem to be going anywhere. The reasons for this are difficult to assess, and certainly many. Torture's "re-emergence" in the United States is actually anything but: torture has never been far away. From its vast presence in the courts of ancient and medieval Europe to its emergent role in intelligence operations in twentieth-century conflicts, torture *persists*. Here is a sample of countries in the twentieth century that are known to have engaged in torture. The list is not complete:

1. Afghanistan
2. Algeria
3. Angola
4. Argentina
5. Brazil
6. Cambodia
7. Chile
8. China
9. Cuba
10. DR Congo
11. Egypt
12. El Salvador
13. England
14. France
15. Georgia
16. Germany
17. Guatemala
18. Haiti
19. Honduras
20. Indonesia
21. Iraq
22. Israel
23. Italy
24. Kenya
25. Mauritania
26. Mexico
27. Morocco
28. Nicaragua
29. Nigeria
30. North Vietnam
31. Paraguay
32. Russia
33. Saudi Arabia
34. Serbia
35. South Africa
36. South Korea
37. South Vietnam
38. Soviet Union
39. Spain
40. Sri Lanka

41. Sudan
42. Syria
43. Thailand
44. Turkey
45. Uganda

46. United States
47. Uruguay
48. Uzbekistan
49. Zimbabwe

Sadly, the defenders of torture persist too. They are greater now, perhaps, than they were 30 years ago—and certainly in more prominent positions. From President George W. Bush and Vice President Dick Cheney to Harvard law professor Alan Dershowitz, these high-profile advocates have at least one thing going for them: they have demanded that we think more carefully and critically than they have yet bothered to do. The results of this reflection are what we have just presented to you in the preceding pages, and their implications are entirely clear: torture, when understood fully and without equivocation, is *never* permissible. It is as base an act as possible. The reasons for its baseness exist aplenty: it defiles everything it touches—both tortured and torturer, as well as the institutions that support and enable these roles to exist.

But the perversion that is torture goes even further. It debases the very things that we pride ourselves on—our ability to communicate with one another, to perform roles in various and novel ways, to utilize technology, and to experience the world as meaning laden. All of these things are turned against themselves; they are distorted in a way that undermines the very existence of their value. Language becomes a mere means of pain implementation, bereft of all real communicative power. Our roles are diminished to the expression of the inhuman humanity of which we are all capable. Technology—the very heart of human civilization—becomes that which proves that civilization is at an end in the torture situation. Meaning itself becomes dictated by another, and the rich phenomenological world in which we exist becomes one haunted by the demons of another's dominance and savagery.

If our analysis has shown anything, it is that the wrongdoing of torture cannot be measured on the scales of utility. The thought experiments designed to generate these artificial calculations are themselves incoherent—they rely on a notion of torture that is utterly empty—that has paid too little attention to the psychological and physical reality of torture. They have paid too little attention to the voices of even the intelligence community—persons who uniformly reject the necessity (and even the utility) of engaging in torture. For those who are interested in exploring our *intuitions*, the unavailability of the ticking-bomb argument, it seems to us, is in itself the end of any powerful argument they might muster.

Of course, if recent government has proven anything, it is that the word "torture" can mean many different things—or, more precisely, it can be *made* to mean many different things. This view is the underlying assumption behind the infamous "torture memo" of 2002. This memo held that an act was torture only if (1) the act resulted in pain equivalent in intensity to organ failure or death, or the act resulted in prolonged mental pain lasting for months and even years, and (2) the act was intended *specifically* to *be* torture.

Thus, in the official policy of the Bush administration, any interrogation that aimed at extracting information was simply ruled out by the memo: the *specific* intent of interrogation is information gathering. Even if it results in prolonged mental pain or severe physical pain, if it isn't *specifically intended* to do so, it cannot be torture. Despite the fact that this memo was later rescinded, it is well known that the policy of the Bush administration remained unchanged. This has been further evidenced by Bush's veto of legislation in March, 2008 that would extend the ban of torture to agents of the United States' Central Intelligence Agency. In explanation, Bush remarked:

> Because the danger remains, we need to ensure our intelligence officials have all they need to stop the terrorists . . . this is no time for Congress to abandon practices that have a proven track record of keeping America safe.[1]

When persons utterly oblivious to the empirical and psychological realities of torture can be at the helm of a nation with immense military power—and perhaps when they lead any nation—the hopes for the abolition of torture seem abysmal. This ignorance reproduces in the idea of "torture lite," as well as in the common distinction between the moral harm done in "physical" and "psychological" torture respectively. But even this distinction—one that we have helped ourselves to, if only for convenience—can itself become part of the very conceptual architecture that aims to legitimate torture. As Uwe Jacobs notes,

> the methodology of so-called "hands-off torture" requires extensive physical manipulation, even though understanding the mechanisms of stress inducement requires psychological knowledge. Thus to think that psychological torture is *not* an assault on the body is a conceptual error from the outset . . . what all torture has in common, regardless of physical or mental appearances, is its assault on the brain. Indeed, *to make a concerted assault on the brain is the primary aim of torture.* ("Documenting the Neurobiology of Psychological Torture," in *The Trauma of Psychological Torture,* 164–165)

This is not a unique view among those investigating the effects of torture on its survivors. Catani, Neuner, Weinbruch, and Elbert, after reviewing several studies of torture survivors, claim that "(1) physical and psychological torture almost always occur simultaneously; and (2) a distinction between these two qualities of torture is unnecessary when discussing the long-term effects on mental health" ("The Tortured Brain," 174).

Indeed, given the obvious *physical* effects of engaging in so-called "psychological torture," Jacobs suggests that the reason we use this phrase at all is twofold. We use the phrase first to convince ourselves that we are "not, in fact, torturing, but acting in a civilized manner by applying 'enhanced interrogation techniques'," and second "to convince the public that what is going on in any given prison does not constitute torture and that no crime has been committed" (167).

But we are not entirely without hope. The force of critical inquiry is too slow, but it is not non-existent. The key to any hope we might have of abolishing torture lies in exposing it for what it is—and in refusing to allow persons to hide in the comfortable confines of their inchoate, malicious intuitions—or, worse still, in their linguistic legerdemain.

This book has been an attempt to move in this direction. We have resisted linguistic sophistry by *acknowledging* the difficulties in defining "torture" adequately. We have thus attempted to explore torture systematically on four different (though sometimes overlapping) models. We have shown that, on each of these models, torture violates the values implicit in all of our actions. We have shown that the standard arguments in favor of torture cannot get off the ground, and hence that the point of departure for the vast majority of those who defend torture must simply be abandoned. We have shown that there are overwhelming reasons for acknowledging that torture is one of the most severe violations of human dignity that is possible. It is by no means a temporary ailment: it *kills* the person subjected to it by fundamentally altering the way the person experiences the world around them. Torture, in essence, robs the tortured of the *human* perspective, and reduces the tortured to one inhabited only by the pain of the past. In the telling locution of Elaine Scarry, torture unmakes the world. But we have not stopped there. Torture is not only a phenomenon of individuals. It is also a phenomenon of institutions. We have explored some of the institutional structures of torture in a way that allows us to deepen our understanding of what makes it morally problematic. As we have argued, the moral depravity of torture has been routinely underestimated by its advocates—something that our analyses have aimed to remedy. It is only by acknowledging torture for what it is that we can ever hope to eradicate it. While we are not confident that eradication is possible, we are confident that even the slightest pretense of hope is better than none—and that even the smallest advance in our collective understanding of torture might well be one step to a world without it.

NOTES

1. COMING TO (DEFINITIONAL) TERMS WITH
TORTURE—FOUR MODELS

1 The torture memo (written by Bybee and Yoo, of the Bush Administration) defines "severe pain" as equal to the pain of organ failure
or death! This will be discussed more fully in Chapter Two.

2 In *The Torture Debate in America*, ed. Karen J. Greenberg.
New York: Cambridge University Press, 2006, p. 317.

3 Tindale, Christopher W. "The Logic of Torture: A Critical Examination," (1996) *Social Theory and Practice*, 22:3, 349–374.

4 Shue, Henry. "Torture," in *Torture: A Collection*, ed. Sanford Levinson.
New York: Oxford University Press, 2004, 47–60.

5 One notable exception is Stephen Kershnar. See his "Objections to
the Systematic Imposition of Punitive Torture," (1999) *International
Journal of Applied Philosophy*, 13:1, 47–56.

6 Amnesty International reports that 75 percent of nations worldwide
engage in torture. Quiroga, J. and Jaranson, J. M. *"Politically-
Motivated Torture and its Survivors: A Desk Study Review of the
Literature," (2005) Torture, 15:(2–3), 39–45.*

7 The nineteenth-century humanists are a tricky case. Voltaire, for
example, maintained that torture was absolutely impermissible
in court proceedings. However, he had no objections to *torture
preable,* the practice of torturing convicted criminals to obtain information about other criminals and crimes. In this respect, the
"absolute" prohibition of torture is anything but.

8 Langbein, John H. *Torture and the Law of Proof: Europe and
England in the Ancient Regime.* Chicago, IL: University Of Chicago
Press, 2006; Langbein, John H. "Torture and the Law of Truth," in
The Phenomenon of Torture, ed. William F. Schulz. Philadelphia,
PA: University of Pennsylvania Press, 2007, 19–26.

9 "Supreme Court of Israel Judgment," in *The Phenomenon of Torture*,
ed. William F. Schulz. Philadelphia, PA: University of Pennsylvania
Press, 2007, 275–283.

10 Gur-Arye, Miriam. "Can the War against Terror Justify the Use
of Force in Interrogations? Reflections in Light of the Israeli Experience," in *Torture: A Collection*, ed. Sanford Levinson. New York:
Oxford University Press, 2004, 183–198.

11 Gross, Oren. "The Prohibition on Torture and the Limits of the
Law," in *Torture: A Collection*, ed. Sanford Levinson. New York:
Oxford University Press, 2004, 229–256.

2. THE ECONOMIC MODEL OF TORTURE—TICKING-BOMB ARGUMENTS AND TORTURE WARRANTS

1 Bentham, Jeremy. "Of Torture," in *The Phenomenon of Torture*, ed. William F. Schulz. Philadelphia, PA: University of Pennsylvania Press, 2007, 221–226.

2 Dershowitz, Alan. "Tortured Reasoning," in *Torture: A Collection*, ed. Sanford Levinson. New York: Oxford University Press, 2004, 257–280 and Dershowitz, Alan. "Why Terrorism Works" in *The Phenomenon of Torture*, ed. William F. Schulz. Philadelphia, PA: University of Pennsylvania Press, 2007, 233–240. Much of this stems from the reasoning of the Israeli Supreme Court, and Dershowitz's dissatisfaction with it. See Supreme Court of Israel. "Judgment Concerning the Legality of the General Security Service's Interrogation Methods" in *Torture: A Collection*, ed. Sanford Levinson. New York: Oxford University Press, 2004, 165–182.

3 Bagaric, Mike and Julie Clarke. *Torture: When the Unthinkable is Morally Permissible.* Albany, NY: State University of New York Press, 2007. Gross, Oren. "The Prohibition on Torture and the Limits of the Law," in *Torture: A Collection*, ed. Sanford Levinson. New York: Oxford University Press, 2004, 229–256; Gur-Arye, Miriam. "Can the War against Terror Justify the Use of Force in Interrogations? Reflections in Light of the Israeli Experience," in *Torture: A Collection*, ed. Sanford Levinson. New York: Oxford University Press, 2004, 183–198; Parry, John T. "Escalation and Necessity: Defining Torture at Home and Abroad," in *Torture: A Collection*, ed. Sanford Levinson. New York: Oxford University Press, 2004, 145–164; Posner, Richard. "Torture, Terrorism, and Interrogation," in *Torture: A Collection*, ed. Sanford Levinson. New York: Oxford University Press, 2004, 291–298. For one recent response to this, see Bufacchi, Vittorio, and Jean-Maria Arrigo. "Terrorism and the State: A Refutation of the Ticking-Bomb Argument," (2006) *Journal of Applied Philosophy*, 23:3, 355–373.

4 McCain's claim is cited in Zimbardo, Philip. *The Lucifer Effect: Understanding How Good People Turn Evil.* New York: Random House, 2007, p. 433.

5 See Scarry, Elaine. "Five Errors in the Reasoning of Alan Dershowitz" in *Torture: A Collection*, ed. Sanford Levinson. New York: Oxford University Press, 2004, 281–290; Gur-Arye, op. cit; Gross op cit.

6 Uwe Steinhoff, "Torture—The Case for Dirty Harry and against Alan Dershowitz," (2006) *Journal of Applied Philosophy*, 23:3, 337–353.

7 We will return to the defense of torture offered in this book in the section titled Further Utilitarian Considerations below.

8 What is interesting about this point in relation to torture, and what Bagaric and Clarke have failed to see, is that torture *does* have a history of abuse within the legal system. We will return to this point later.

9 Shue, Henry. "Torture," in *Torture: A Collection*, ed. Sanford Levinson. New York: Oxford University Press, 2004, 47–60.

10 Levinson, Sanford (ed.). *Torture: A Collection*. Oxford: Oxford University Press, 2004, p. 28.

11 Twining and Paskins offer several nice examples of hard cases. Twining, William and Barrie Paskins. "Torture and Philosophy," (1978) *Aristotelian Society*, 52: 143–168.

12 See Kois, Lisa M. "Dance, Sister, Dance!" in *An End to Torture: Strategies for Its Eradication*, ed. Bertil Dunér. New York: Zed Books, 1998 and Claudia Card, "Torture in Ordinary Circumstances," in *Moral Psychology: Feminist Ethics and Social Theory*, ed. Peggy DesAutels and Margaret Urban Walker. New York: Rowman & Littlefield Publishers, Inc., 2004.

13 This claim is meant to be acceptable to both realists and anti-realists in mathematics. Even if "triangles" are just human constructions that arise out of our complicated form of life, they are such as to be regarded by us as having their qualities independently of our particular beliefs, desires, and individual actions.

14 Thomson, Judith Jarvis. "A Defense of Abortion," (1971) *Philosophy & Public Affairs*, 1:1, Collected in *Ethics: History, Theory, and Contemporary Issues,* ed. Steven Cahn and Peter Markie. Oxford: Oxford University Press, 2002, 739–750.

15 To remind the reader of the details of this case:

> You wake up one morning and find yourself back to back in bed with an unconscious violinist. A famous unconscious violinist. He has been found to have a fatal kidney ailment, and the Society of Music Lovers has canvassed all the available medical records and found that you alone have the right blood type to help. They have therefore kidnapped you, and last night the violinist's circulatory system was plugged into yours, so that your kidneys can be used to extract poisons from his blood as well as your own. (740)

Thomson, Judith Jarvis "A Defense of Abortion," in *Ethics: History, Theory, and Contemporary Issues*, ed. Steven Cahn and Peter Markie. Oxford: Oxford University Press, 2002, 739–750, p. 740.

16 P. 41, *Kubark Interrogation Manual, 1963*. Available through ACLU.

17 Bagaric, Mike and Julie Clarke. *Torture: When the Unthinkable is Morally Permissible*. Albany, NY: State University of New York Press, 2007.

18 Dershowitz, Alan "Tortured Reasoning," in *Torture: A Collection,* ed. Sanford Levinson. Oxford and New York: Oxford University Press, 2004. Portions of the article included in this collection were first published as chapter 4 of Dershowitz's *Why Terrorism Works: Understanding the Threat, Responding to the Challenge*. New Haven and London: Yale University Press, 2002. In what follows, we will cite both versions of this material, as some of Dershowitz's arguments

are more effectively, or more thoroughly, stated in one publication rather than another. We will use abbreviations of titles (TR for Tortured Reasoning and WTW for Why Terrorism Works) to make clear which version is being cited. It should also be noted that Dershowitz has promoted this view in numerous newspaper articles, as well as on network television. Hence its importance.

19 And Dershowitz is well aware of this. He lists five alternative choices in responding to torture (though one in a footnote) in WTW, see chapter 4, 149–150, and note 25, 251.

20 Bufacchi, Vittorio and Jean Maria Arrigo, "Terrorism, and the State: a Refutation of the Ticking-Bomb Argument," (2006) *Journal of Applied Philosophy,* 23:3.

21 See, for example, Sung, C. "Torturing the Ticking-Bomb Terrorist: an Analysis of Judicially Sanctioned Torture in the Context of Terrorism," (2003) *Boston College Third World Law Journal,* 23, 193–212.

22 Uwe Steinhoff has recently raised this objection, albeit without reference to incentive talk. As Steinhoff points out, although Dershowitz thinks these two examples support his case,

> [w]hat his examples show (if they show anything) is that an attorney general who is *authorized* to put a wiretap without judicial warrant is more likely to put a wiretap than an attorney general who does need a warrant. However, the question to be answered is whether torture would be *less likely* under a requirement of a judicial warrant than *under a total ban* (347).

See "Torture—The Case for Dirty Harry and against Alan Dershowitz," (2006) *Journal of Applied Philosophy,* 23:3.

23 Dershowitz relies, as we do, on John H. Langbein's work—in particular, his *Torture and the Law of Proof: Europe and England in the Ancient Regime.* Chicago, IL: Chicago University Press, 2006. For a condensed overview of the legal proceeding surrounding torture, see Langbein, "The Legal History of Torture," in *Torture: A Collection,* ed. Sanford Levinson. Oxford and New York: Oxford University Press, 2004.

24 See *Torture: A Collection,* ed. Sanford Levinson. Oxford and New York: Oxford University Press, 2004.

25 Resolution of Advice and Consent to Ratification of the Convention against Torture and Other Forms of Cruel, Inhuman or Degrading Treatment or Punishment: Reservations, Declarations, and Under-standings, part II (1)(a), 136 Cong. Rec S17491 (daily edition October 27, 1990).

26 Parry, John T. "Escalation and Necessity: Defining Torture at Home and Abroad" in *Torture: A Collection,* ed. Sanford Levinson. Oxford and New York: Oxford University Press, 2004.

27 These results have been usefully summarized in Hathaway, Oona. "The Promise and Limits of the International Law of Torture" in

Torture: A Collection, ed. Sanford Levinson. Oxford and New York: Oxford University Press, 2004.

28 Statistics obviously admit of quite a range, some of which can be accounted for by the time and place of the polling. One poll, discussed below, puts the percentage of Americans that accept torture under some circumstances at 61 percent (another, also discussed below, puts the percentage at 36!).

29 These worries are raised by many, not the least of whom include: Judge Richard A. Posner, "Torture, Terrorism, and Interrogation," and Professor Elaine Scarry, "Five Errors in the Reasoning of Alan Dershowitz," in *Torture: A Collection,* ed. Sanford Levinson. Oxford and New York: Oxford University Press, 2004.

Dershowitz claims that Scarry's response (that we should decide about the fate of a torturer *after* the fact—there should be no policy for engaging in torture) is inadequate. He seems to conflate two positions: (1) having no policy regarding torture, and (2) having a "decide on the ground" policy. He attributes (2) to Scarry, which he then rightly criticizes—but this is not Scarry's view. Her view, rather, is (1). See her response to Dershowitz, *op. cit.*

30 "Poll Finds Broad Approval of Terrorist Torture," Americas, MSNBC.com, http://www.msnbc.msn.com/id/10345320/ Last consulted 17 August 2007. It should be noted, of course, that other polls put the percentage of Americans approving of torture much lower. We will discuss this below.

31 "One-Third Support Torture," BBC News, http://news.bbc.co.uk/1/hi/in_depth/6063386.stm#table Last accessed on 17 August 2007.

3. THE PHENOMENOLOGICAL MODEL OF TORTURE— DIGNITY AND THE DESTRUCTION OF AGENCY

1 This view is forcefully defended in Sussman, 2005. We will explore Sussman's important work in much more detail below.

2 See *At the Side of Torture Survivors: Treating a Terrible Assault on Human Dignity,* ed. Sep Graessner, M. D., Norbert Gurris, and Christian Pross, M. D. Baltimore, MD: Johns Hopkins University Press, 2001; and Gerrity, Ellen, Terrence M. Keane, Farris Tuma, and Sister Dianna Ortiz. "Future Directions," in *The Mental Health Consequences of Torture,* eds Ellen Gerrity, Terrence M. Keane, and Farris Tuma. New York: Springer, 2001, 335–342.

3 The expression is from Elaine Scarry's brilliant book, *The Body in Pain: The Making and Unmaking of the World.* New York: Oxford University Press, 1985.

4 Becker, Ernest. *The Denial of Death.* New York: Simon and Schuster, 1973.

5 For a detailed account of Kant along these lines, see Wisnewski, J. Jeremy. *Wittgenstein and Ethical Inquiry: A Defense of Ethics as Clarification.* London: Continuum, 2007.
See in particular chapter 2.

6 This is precisely why Wittgenstein thought that it was silly to attempt to prove the existence of the external world: no evidence could possibly be as secure as the certainty it aimed to justify. See *On Certainty.*

7 For a defense of this, see Jeff MacMahan, *The Ethics of Killing.*

8 For one argument against this kind of skepticism, see Wisnewski and Jacoby, "Failures of Sight: An Argument for Moral Perception," *American Philosophical Quarterly,* 2007.

9 Levinas, Emmanuel. *Totality and Infinity.* Trans. Alphonso Lingis. Pittsburgh, PA: Duquesne University Press, 1969.

10 Casey, Lee A. and David B. Rivkin, Jr, "Rethinking the Geneva Conventions," in *The Torture Debate in America,* ed. Karen J. Greenberg. New York: Cambridge University Press, 2006, 203–213.

11 While we think this is in the spirit of the Kantian argument, it differs in the details.

4. THE DRAMATURGICAL MODEL—INTERROGATION'S IMMORALITY PLAY

1 As You Like It. Act II, Scene 7.

2 See Eliot Freidson, (July 1983) *Contemporary Sociology,* 12:4, 359–362.

3 Charon, Joel M. *Symbolic Interactionism: An Introduction, an Interpretation, an Integration.* Upper Saddle River, NJ: Prentice Hall, 2007.

4 See Edward Lemert, *Human Deviance, Social Problems, and Social Control,* Prentice-Hall, 1972, 18. See also Greg Smith, *Erving Goffman,* Routledge 2006, 103.

5 When we review the different institutions in our Western society, we find some that are encompassing to a degree discontinuously greater than the ones next in line. Their encompassing or total character is symbolized by the barrier to social intercourse with the outside and to departure that is often built right into the physical plant, such as locked doors, high walls, barbed wire, cliffs, water, forests, or moors. (Goffman, *Asylums,* 4).

6 http://www.amnestyusa.org/denounce_torture/statement_on_interrogation.pdf accessed July 5, 2008.

7 FM 2–22.3, Human Intelligence Collector Operations, 8.1, September 2006.

8 Cited by Jean Maria Arrigo at International Society for Military Ethics, University of San Diego, 2008.

5. THE COMMUNICATIVE MODEL OF TORTURE— UNDERSTANDING INSTITUTIONALLY PERMISSIVE TORTURE

1 Tim Golden, "In U.S. Report, Brutal Details of 2 Afghan Inmates' Deaths" (May 20, 2005) *New York Times,* A1.

2 These two conditions connect with the *Explanatory–Diagnostic* and *Anticipatory–Utopian* aspects of Critical Theory. See Seyla Benhabib, *Critique, Norm, Utopia: A Study of the Foundations of Critical Theory*. New York: Columbia University Press, 1986, 225–226. They might also connect in the wider tradition of Critical Theory to what Benhabib calls the *context of genesis* and *context of application*. See Ibid., 281.

3 Again, our interest is not to argue for or against the thesis that strategic action is parasitic on communicative action or for the conceptual foundations of the Habermasian speech–act taxonomy. We'll presuppose that both are warranted moves and we want merely to say how these categories might help us think about situations of interrogation, especially the ways in which controlled interrogations can degenerate into violence.

4 Interrogators spent a lot of time learning how to interpret non-verbal cues.

5 Bohman, James. "Distorted Communication: Formal Pragmatics as a Critical Theory" in Lewis Hahn, Perspectives on Habermas. Peru, IL: Open Court Publishing, 2000, 3–20.

6 See Benhabib, 285.

7 It is for this reason that we could plausibly construe the interrogation setting itself as an institutionally formed locus of "distorted communication."

8 From the Mora Memo.

9 From the Mora Memo of 2004, a part of the "Church Report."

10 One striking feature of the coercive pressures that interrogators used against detainees, aside from the case of Dilawar, was that they were not *overtly* brutal.

11 CIA: *KUBARK Manual*. Government Document, 1963. Available through ACLU, pp. 88, 90, 94.

12 *Human Resource Exploitation Training Manual*—1983, June 8, 1988 (Box 1 CIA Training Manuals, Folder: Resource Exploitation Training Manual, National Security Archive, Washington), I-D.] pg. 8 Mackey did this with "Somalie Bob" and others, telling them that they "had no choice" but to send them to Cuba, etc.

13 In *The Torture Debate in America*, ed. Karen J. Greenberg. New York: Cambridge University Press, 2006, pg. 317

14 There are, indeed, other ways in which lifeworld crises manifested themselves in this case. Next, at the level of social integration, a kind of "anomie" emerged, if that is taken to be a lack of "law or ethical standard." The above crisis of loss of meaning and legitimation meant that each successive interrogation unit interpreted Army doctrine more and more liberally—which created escalating risk of violence. Thus, we have a kind of anomie, understood in terms of a loss of rule of law.

15 Budiansky, "Intelligence: Truth Extraction."

6. ASSESSING THE VARIETIES OF TORTURE—CONCLUDING REFLECTIONS ON A RECURRENT PROBLEM

1 Lee Meyes, Steven and Mark Mazzetti, "Bush Vetoes a Bill on CIA Tactics, Affirms Legacy," (March 9, 2008) *New York Times,* A1.

BIBLIOGRAPHY

LEGAL AND MILITARY DOCUMENTS

Commentary on the United Nations Convention on the Rights of the Child, Article 37: Prohibition of Torture, Death Penalty, Life Imprisonment and Deprivation of Liberty. Brill Academic Publishers, 2006.

Conclusions and Recommendations of the UN Committee against Torture: Eleventh to Twenty-Second Sessions (1993–1999) (Raoul Wallenberg Institute Series of Intergovernmental Human Rights Documentation). New York: Springer, 2000.

Essential Handbook for KGB Agents, London: Industrial Information Index, XXXX.

"Memorandum for Alberto R. Gonzales, Counsel to the President from US Department of Justice, Office of Legal Counsel," in *Civil Liberties vs. National Security in a Post-9/11 World,* eds Darmer, M. Katherine B., Robert M. Baird and Stuart E. Rosenbaum. Amherst, NY: Prometheus Books, 2004, 303–316.

CIA: Human Resource Exploitation Training Manual, Government Document, 1983. Available through ACLU.

CIA: KUBARK Manual. Government Document, 1963. Available through ACLU.

Habeas Corpus Statute: "28 United States Code, Section 2241. Power to Grant Writ," in *Civil Liberties vs. National Security in a Post-9/11 World,* eds Darmer, M. Katherine B., Robert M. Baird and Stuart E. Rosenbaum. Amherst, NY: Prometheus Books, 2004, 49–53.

"Landau Commission Report," in *The Phenomenon of Torture,* ed. William F. Schulz. Philadelphia, PA: University of Pennsylvania Press, 2007, 267–274.

ADDITIONAL SOURCES

Abbott, Geoffrey. *Execution.* New York: St. Martin's Press, 2005.

Aceves, William J. *Anatomy of Torture: A Documentary History of Filartiga v. Pena Irala.* Boston, MA: Brill Academy Publishers, 2007.

Ahmad, Salah. "The Healing Power of Storytelling," in *At the Side of Torture Survivors: Treating a Terrible Assault on Human Dignity,* eds Sep Graessner, M. D., Norbert Gurris, and Christian Pross, M. D. Baltimore, MD: Johns Hopkins University Press, 2001, 112–125.

Allhoff, Fritz. "A Defense of Torture: Separation of Cases, Ticking Time-bombs, and Moral Justification," (2005) *International Journal of Applied Philosophy,* 19:2, 243–264.

Allhoff, Fritz. "Terrorism and Torture," (2003) *International Journal of Applied Philosophy*, 17:1, 121–134.

Americas, "Poll Finds Broad Approval of Terrorist Torture," MSNBC. com, http://www.msnbc.msn.com/id/10345320/ Last consulted 17 August 2007.

Améry, Jean. *At the Mind's Limits: Contemplations by a Survivor.* Bloomington and Indianapolis, IN: Indiana University Press, 1980.

Amery, Jean. "Torture," in *The Phenomenon of Torture*, ed. William F. Schulz. Philadelphia, PA: University of Pennsylvania Press, 2007, 80–87.

Amnesty International. "International Criminal Court Q&A Sheet," in *The Phenomenon of Torture*, ed. William F. Schulz. Philadelphia, PA: University of Pennsylvania Press, 2007, 308–310.

Amnesty International. "Police Officers Convicted of Torturing a Man in Detention," in *The Phenomenon of Torture*, ed. William F. Schulz. Philadelphia, PA: University of Pennsylvania Press, 2007, 297–298.

Amnesty International. *Report on Torture*. New York: Farrar, Straus and Giroux, 1975.

Amnesty International: "Report Uzbekistan," in *The Phenomenon of Torture*, ed. William F. Schulz. Philadelphia, PA: University of Pennsylvania Press, 2007, 95–96.

Amnesty International. *Torture Worldwide: An Affront to Human Dignity*. New York: Amnesty International, 2000.

Anderson, Craig A. and Nicholas L. Carnagey. "Violent Evil and the General Aggression Model," in *The Social Psychology of Good and Evil*, ed. Arthur G. Miller. New York: The Guilford Press, 2005, 168–192.

Aoilain, Fionnuala Ni. "The European Convention on Human Rights and Its Prohibition on Torture," in *Torture: A Collection*, ed. Sanford Levinson. New York: Oxford University Press, 2004, 213–228.

Arendt, Hannah. "The Origins of Totalitarianism," in *The Phenomenon of Torture*, ed. William F. Schulz. Philadelphia, PA: University of Pennsylvania Press, 2007, 196–200.

Aronson, Elliot. "Reducing Hostility and Building Compassion: Lessons from the Jigsaw Classroom," in *The Social Psychology of Good and Evil*, ed. Arthur G. Miller. New York: The Guilford Press, 2005, 469–488.

Arrigo, Jean Maria and Ray Bennett, "Organizational Supports for Abusive Interrogations in the 'War on Terror'," (November 2007) *Peace and Conflict: Journal of Peace Psychology*, 13:4, 411–421.

Arrigo, Jean Maria and Richard V. Wagner, "Psychologists and Military Interrogators Rethink the Psychology of Torture," (November 2007) *Peace and Conflict: Journal of Peace Psychology*, 13:4, 393–398.

Ask, Ingrid, Juan Almendares Bonilla, Terence Dowdall, Ümit Erkol, and Selim Ölçer. "Treatment Centres in Torturing States," in *An End to Torture: Strategies for Its Eradication*, ed. Dunér, Bertil. New York: St. Martin's Press, 1999, 154–171.

Athey, Stephanie. "Rethinking Torture's Dark Chamber," (2008) *Peace Review: A Journal of Social Justice,* 20, 13–21.

Atkinson, Keith. "The Torturer's Tale," in *The Phenomenon of Torture*, ed. William F. Schulz. Philadelphia, PA: University of Pennsylvania Press, 2007, 104–109.

Bagaric, Mike and Julie Clarke. *Torture: When the Unthinkable is Morally Permissible*. Albany, NY: State University of New York Press, 2007.

Baier, Annette C. "Violent Demonstrations," in *Violence, Terrorism, and Justice*, eds R. G. Frey and Christopher W. Morris. Cambridge: Cambridge University Press, 1991, 33–58.

Bartlett, Robert. *Trial by Fire and Water: The Medieval Judicial Ordeal*. Oxford: Oxford University Press, 1986.

Başoğlu, Metin, Maria Livanou, and Cvetana Crnobarić. "Torture vs Other Cruel, Inhuman, and Degrading Treatment: Is the Distinction Real or Apparent?" (2007) *Arch Gen Psychiatry*, 64:March, 277–285.

Başoğlu, Metin, James M. Jaranson, Richard Mollica, and Marriane Kastrup. "Torture and Mental Health: A Research Overview," in *The Mental Health Consequences of Torture*, eds Ellen Gerrity, Terrence M. Keane, and Farris Tuma. New York: Springer, 2001, 35–64.

Bassiouni, M. Cherif. "Great Nations and Torture," in *The Torture Debate in America*, ed. Karen J. Greenberg. New York: Cambridge University Press, 2006, 256–260.

Baumeister, Roy F. and Aaron Beck. *Evil: Inside Human Violence and Cruelty*. New York: Owl Books, 1999.

BBC News, "One-Third Support Torture," http://news.bbc.co.uk/1/hi/in_depth/6063386.stm#table (accessed on August 17, 2007).

Beccaria, Cesare. "An Essay on Crimes and Punishments," in *The Phenomenon of Torture*, ed. William F. Schulz. Philadelphia, PA: University of Pennsylvania Press, 2007, 34–35.

Becker, Ernest. *The Denial of Death*. New York: Simon and Schuster, 1973.

Beebe, Gilbert. "Follow Up Studies of World War II and Korean Prisoners," (1970) *American Journal of Epidemiology*, 92:2, 400.

Benhabib, Seyla. *Critique, Norm, Utopia: A Study of the Foundations of Critical Theory*. New York: Columbia University Press, 1986.

Bennett, Ray. "Endorsement by the Seminar Military Interrogators," (November 2007) *Peace and Conflict: Journal of Peace Psychology*, 13:4, 391–392.

Bentham, Jeremy. "Of Torture," in *The Phenomenon of Torture*, ed. William F. Schulz. Philadelphia, PA: University of Pennsylvania Press, 2007, 221–226.

Benvenisti, Meron. "An Old Refrain that Stabs at the Heart," in *Abu Ghraib: The Politics of Torture*. ed. Anonymously with the support of the Society for the Study of Native Arts and Sciences. Berkeley, CA: North Atlantic Books, 2004, 56–59.

Berger, Peter. "Sociological Perspectives—Life as Drama," in *Life as Theatre: A Dramaturgical Sourcebook*. 2nd edn, ed. Dennis Brisset and Charles Edgley. New York: Aldine de Gruyter, 1990, 51–62.

Bernstein, Richard. "Kidnapping has Germans Debating Police Torture," in *The Phenomenon of Torture*, ed. William F. Schulz. Philadelphia, PA: University of Pennsylvania Press, 2007, 230–232.

Bilder, Richard B. and Detlev F. Vagts. "Speaking Law to Power: Lawyers and Torture," in *The Torture Debate in America*, ed. Karen J. Greenberg. New York: Cambridge University Press, 2006, 151–161.

Blumer, Herbert. *Symbolic Interactionism: Perspective and Method*. Berkeley, CA: University of California Press, 1969.

Bob, Brecher. *Torture and the Ticking Bomb*. Malden and Oxford: Blackwell Publishing, 2007.

Bohman, James. "Distorted Communication: Formal Pragmatics as a Critical Theory" in Lewis Hahn, Perspectives on Habermas. Peru, IL: Open Court Publishing, 2000, 3–20.

Booth, Cherie. "Sexual Violence, Torture, and International Justice," in *Torture: Does it Make Us Safer? Is It Ever OK? A Human Rights Perspective*, eds Kenneth Roth and Minky Worden. New York: The New Press and Human Rights Watch, 2005, 117–130.

Boulesbaa, Ahcene. *The U. N. Convention on Torture and the Prospects for Enforcement (International Studies in Human Rights)*. New York: Springer, 1999.

Bowden, Mark. "The Dark Art of Interrogation," (2003) *The Atlantic Monthly*, October, 51–76.

Bowker, David W. "Unwise Counsel: The War on Terrorism and the Criminal Mistreatment of detainees in U.S. Custody," in *The Torture Debate in America*, ed. Karen J. Greenberg. New York: Cambridge University Press, 2006, 183–202.

Brisset, Dennis and Edgley, Charles (eds). *Life as Theatre: A Dramaturgical Sourcebook, 2nd edn*. New York: Aldine de Gruyter, 1990.

Brody, Reed. "The Road to Abu Ghraib: Torture and Impunity in U.S. Detention," in *Torture: Does it Make Us Safer? Is It Ever OK? A Human Rights Perspective*, eds Kenneth Roth and Minky Worden. New York: The New Press and Human Rights Watch, 2005, 145–154.

Brownlie, Ian and Guy S. Goodwin-Gill. *Basic Documents on Human Rights*. New York: Oxford University Press, 2002.

Brownmiller, Susan. "Against Our Will," in *The Phenomenon of Torture*, ed. William F. Schulz. Philadelphia, PA: University of Pennsylvania Press, 2007, 88–94.

Budiansky, Stephen. "Intelligence: Truth Extraction," (2005) *The Atlantic Monthly*, June, 32–35.

Bufacchi, Vittorio and Jean-Maria Arrigo. "Terrorism and the State: A Refutation of the Ticking-Bomb Argument," (2006) *Journal of Applied Philosophy*, 23:3, 355–373.

Bybee, Jay. "The Torture Memo," in *The Torture Debate in America*, ed. Karen J. Greenberg. New York: Cambridge University Press, 2006, 317–357.

Card, Claudia. "Rape as a Terrorist Institution," in *Violence, Terrorism, and Justice*, eds R. G. Frey and Christopher W. Morris. Cambridge: Cambridge University Press, 1991, 296–319.

Card, Claudia. *The Atrocity Paradigm: A Theory of Evil.* New York: Oxford University Press, 2002.

Card, Claudia. "Ticking Bombs and Interrogations," (2008) *Criminal Law and Philosophy,* 2:1, 1–15.

Card, Claudia. "Torture in Ordinary Circumstances," in *Moral Psychology: Feminist Ethics and Social Theory,* eds Peggy DesAutels and Margaret Urban Walker. New York: Rowman and Littlefield Publishers, Inc., 2004.

Carlson, Eric Stener. *The Pear Tree: Is Torture Ever Justified?* Atlanta: Clarity Press, 2006.

Caron, David D. "If Afghanistan Has Failed, Then Afghanistan is Dead: "Failed States" and the Inappropriate Substitution of Legal Conclusion for Political Description," in *The Torture Debate in America,* ed. Karen J. Greenberg. New York: Cambridge University Press, 2006, 214–222.

Casey, Lee A. and David B. Rivkin, Jr, "Rethinking the Geneva Conventions," in *The Torture Debate in America,* ed. Karen J. Greenberg. New York: Cambridge University Press, 2006, 203–213.

Cassese, Antonio. *Inhuman States: Imprisonment, Detention and Torture in Europe Today.* Cambridge, UK and Boston, MA: Polity Press, 1996.

Catani, Claudia, Frank Neuner, Christian Wienbruch, and Thomas Elbert. "The Tortured Brain," in *The Trauma of Psychological Torture,* ed. Almerindo E. Ojeda. Westport, CT: Praeger, 2008, 173–188.

Chaliand, Gérard, and Arnaud Blin. *The History of Terrorism: From Antiquity to al Qaeda.* California: University of California Press, 2007.

Charon, Joel M. *Symbolic Interactionism: An Introduction, an Interpretation, an Integration.* Upper Saddle River, NJ: Prentice Hall, 2007.

Chicago Tribune Editorial. "Erring on Enemy Combatants," in *Civil Liberties vs. National Security in a Post-9/11 World,* eds M. Darmer, B. Katherine, Robert M. Baird and Stuart E. Rosenbaum. Amherst, NY: Prometheus Books, 2004, 299–302.

Chriss, James. "Habermas, Goffman, and Communicative Action: Implications for Professional Practice," (1995) *American Sociological Review,* 60:4, 545–565.

Claude, Richard Pierre. "Filartiga v. Pena-Irala," in *The Phenomenon of Torture,* ed. William F. Schulz. Philadelphia, PA: University of Pennsylvania Press, 2007, 325–332.

Cohen, Richard. "A Plunge from the Moral Heights," in *Civil Liberties vs. National Security in a Post-9/11 World,* eds M. Darmer, B. Katherine, Robert M. Baird and Stuart E. Rosenbaum. Amherst, NY: Prometheus Books, 2004, 317–320.

Conroy, John. *Unspeakable Acts, Ordinary People: The Dynamics of Torture.* Berkeley, CA: University of California Press, 2000.

Copelon, Rhonda. "Intimate Terror," in *The Phenomenon of Torture,* ed. William F. Schulz. Philadelphia, PA: University of Pennsylvania Press, 2007, 180–193.

Cowan, Geoffrey. "Reporters and Rhetoric," in *What Orwell Didn't Know: Propaganda and the New Face of American Politics*, ed. András Szántó. New York: Public Affairs, 2007, 158–165.

Crelinston, Ronald. "How to Make a Torturer," in *The Phenomenon of Torture*, ed. William F. Schulz. Philadelphia, PA: University of Pennsylvania Press, 2007, 210–214.

Crelinsten, Ronald. "In Their Own Words," in *The Phenomenon of Torture*, ed. William F. Schulz. Philadelphia, PA: University of Pennsylvania Press, 2007, 141–154.

Curzer, Howard J. "Admirable Immorality, Dirty Hands, Ticking Bombs, and Torturing Innocents," (2006) *The Southern Journal of Philosophy*, XLIV, 31–56.

Danner, Mark. "The Logic of Torture," in *Abu Ghraib: The Politics of Torture*. ed. Anonymously with support of the Society for the Study of Native Arts and Sciences. Berkeley, CA: North Atlantic Books, 2004, 17–46.

Danner, Mark. *Torture and Truth: America, Abu Ghraib, and the War on Terror*. New York: New York Review Books, 2004.

Danner, Mark. "Torture and Truth," in *Abu Ghraib: The Politics of Torture*. ed. Anonymously with support of the Society for the Study of Native Arts and Sciences. Berkeley, CA: North Atlantic Books, 2004, 1–16.

Danner, Mark. "Words in a Time of War: On Rhetoric, Truth, and Power," in *What Orwell Didn't Know: Propaganda and the New Face of American Politics*, ed. András Szántó. New York: Public Affairs, 2007, 16–36.

Darmer, M. Katherine B., Robert M. Baird and Stuart E. Rosenbaum (eds) *Civil Liberties vs. National Security in a Post-9/11 World*. Amherst, NY: Prometheus Books, 2004.

Davis, Michael. "The Moral Justifiability of Torture and other Cruel, Inhuman, or Degrading Treatment," (2005) *International Journal of Applied Philosophy*, 19:2, 161–178.

Department of the Army. *U.S. Army Intelligence and Interrogation Handbook: The Official Guide on Prisoner Interrogation*. Guilford, DE: The Lyons Press, 2005.

Dershowitz, Alan M. *Preemption: A Knife that Cuts Both Ways*. New York: W.W. Norton and Company, 2006.

Dershowitz, Alan M. "Should the Ticking Bomb Terrorist Be Tortured? A Case Study in How a Democracy Should Make Tragic Choices," in *Civil Liberties vs. National Security in a Post-9/11 World*, eds M. Darmer, B. Katherine, Robert M. Baird and Stuart E. Rosenbaum. Amherst, NY: Prometheus Books, 2004, 189–214.

Dershowitz, Alan. "Tortured Reasoning," in *Torture: A Collection*, ed. Sanford Levinson. New York: Oxford University Press, 2004, 257–280.

Dershowitz, Alan. "Why Terrorism Works" in *The Phenomenon of Torture*, ed. William F. Schulz. Philadelphia, PA: University of Pennsylvania Press, 2007, 233–240.

Dershowitz, Alan. *Why Terrorism Works: Understanding the Threat, Responding to the Challenge.* New Haven, CT: Yale University Press, 2002.

Dinh, Viet D. "Freedom and Security after September 11," in *Civil Liberties vs. National Security in a Post-9/11 World*, eds M. Darmer, B. Katherine, Robert M. Baird and Stuart E. Rosenbaum. Amherst, NY: Prometheus Books, 2004, 105–114.

Dorf, Michael C. "Renouncing Torture," in *The Torture Debate in America*, ed. Karen J. Greenberg. New York: Cambridge University Press, 2006, 247–252.

Dratel, Joshua. "The Curious Debate," in *The Torture Debate in America*, ed. Karen J. Greenberg. New York: Cambridge University Press, 2006, 111–117.

Drolshagen, Jon. "The Winter Soldier Investigation," in *The Phenomenon of Torture*, ed. William F. Schulz. Philadelphia, PA: University of Pennsylvania Press, 2007, 132–135.

Drumbl, Mark A. *Atrocity, Punishment, and International Law.* Cambridge: Cambridge University Press, 2007.

Dubensky, Joyce S. and Rachel Lavery. "Torture: An Interreligious Debate," in *The Torture Debate in America*, ed. Karen J. Greenberg. New York: Cambridge University Press, 2006, 162–181.

DuBois, Marc. "Human Rights Education for the Police," in *The Phenomenon of Torture*, ed. William F. Schulz. Philadelphia, PA: University of Pennsylvania Press, 2007, 347–356.

DuBois, Page. "Torture and Truth," in *The Phenomenon of Torture*, ed. William F. Schulz. Philadelphia, PA: University of Pennsylvania Press, 2007, 13–15.

Dunér, Bertil. *An End to Torture: Strategies for Its Eradication.* New York: St. Martin's Press, 1999.

Dunér, Bertil. "Atrocities by Non-state Actors," in *An End to Torture: Strategies for Its Eradication*, ed. Dunér, Bertil. St. Martin's Press, 1999, 109–132.

Edgerton, Robert B. and Keith F. Otterbein. *The Worldwide Practice of Torture: A Preliminary Report.* Lewiston, NY: Edwin Mellen Pr, 2007.

Ehrenrich, Barbara. "Feminism's Assumptions Upended," in *Abu Ghraib: The Politics of Torture.* ed. Anonymously with support of the Society for the Study of Native Arts and Sciences. Berkeley, CA: North Atlantic Books, 2004, 65–70.

Eisenberg, Nancy, Carlos Valiente, and Claire Champion. "Empathy-Related Responding: Moral, Social, and Socialization Correlates," in *The Social Psychology of Good and Evil*, ed. Arthur G. Miller. New York: The Guilford Press, 2005, 386–416.

Elsass, Peter. *Treating Victims of Torture and Violence: Theoretical, Cross-Cultural, and Clinical Implications.* New York: New York University Press, 1997.

Elshtain, Jean Bethke. "Reflection on the Problem of 'Dirty Hands'," in *Torture: A Collection*, ed. Sanford Levinson. New York: Oxford University Press, 2004, 77–92.

Engdahl, Brian and John A. Fairbank. "Former Prisoners of War: Highlights of Empirical Research," in *The Mental Health Consequences of Torture*, eds Gerrity, Ellen, Terrence M. Keane, and Farris Tuma. New York: Springer, 2001, 133–142.

European Court of Human Rights. *Aydin vs. Turkey*, in *The Phenomenon of Torture*, ed. William F. Schulz. Philadelphia, PA: University of Pennsylvania Press, 2007, 304–307.

Evans, Malcolm D. and Rod Morgan. "Preventing Torture," in *The Phenomenon of Torture*, ed. William F. Schulz. Philadelphia, PA: University of Pennsylvania Press, 2007, 38–48.

Evans, Malcolm D. and Rod Morgan. *Preventing Torture: A Study of the European Convention for the Prevention of Torture and Inhuman or Degrading Treatment or Punishment*. Oxford: Oxford University Press, 1998.

Fabri, Dr. Mary R. "Treating Torture Victims," in *Torture: Does it Make Us Safer? Is It Ever OK? A Human Rights Perspective*, eds Kenneth Roth and Minky Worden. New York: The New Press and Human Rights Watch, 2005, 131–135.

Fairbank, John A., Matthew J. Friedman, and Metin Başoğlu. "Psychosocial Models," in *The Mental Health Consequences of Torture*, eds Gerrity, Ellen, Terrence M. Keane, and Farris Tuma. New York: Springer, 2001, 65–72.

Fairbank, John A., Matthew J. Friedman, and Steven Southwick. "Veterans of Armed Conflicts," in *The Mental Health Consequences of Torture*, eds Gerrity, Ellen, Terrence M. Keane, Farris Tuma. New York: Springer, 2001, 121–132.

Fassihi, Farnaz. "Lessons from the War Zone," in *What Orwell Didn't Know: Propaganda and the New Face of American Politics*, ed. Szántó, András. New York: Public Affairs, 2007, 166–174.

Feitlowitz, Marguerite. *A Lexicon of Terror: Argentina and the Legacies of Torture*. Oxford: Oxford University Press, 1999.

Feldman, Noah. "Ugly Americans," in *The Torture Debate in America*, ed. Karen J. Greenberg. New York: Cambridge University Press, 2006, 267–282.

Fellner, Jamie. "Torture in U.S. Prisons," in *Torture: Does it Make Us Safer? Is It Ever OK? A Human Rights Perspective*, eds Kenneth Roth and Minky Worden. New York: The New Press and Human Rights Watch, 2005, 173–183.

Felner, Eitan. "Torture and Terrorism: Painful Lessons from Israel," in *Torture: Does it Make Us Safer? Is It Ever OK? A Human Rights Perspective*, eds Kenneth Roth and Minky Worden. New York: The New Press and Human Rights Watch, 2005, 28–43.

Fiala, Andrew. "A Critique of Exceptions: Torture, Terrorism, and the Lesser Evil Argument," (2006) *International Journal of Applied Philosophy*, 20:1, 127–142.

Fields, Rona M. "The Neurobiological Consequences of Psychological Torture," in *The Trauma of Psychological Torture*, ed. Almerindo E. Ojeda. Westport, CT: Praeger, 2008, 139–162.

Fiske, Susan T. "What's in a Category?: Responsibility, Intent, and the Avoidability of Bias Against Outgroups," in *The Social Psychology of Good and Evil*, ed. Arthur G. Miller. New York: The Guilford Press, 2005, 127–140.

Fitzgerald, Frances. "Stellar Spin," in *What Orwell Didn't Know: Propaganda and the New Face of American Politics*, ed. Szántó, András. New York: Public Affairs, 2007, 87–96.

FM 2–22.3, Human Intelligence Collector Operations, 8.1, September 2006.

Foucault, Michel. "Discipline and Punish," in *The Phenomenon of Torture*, ed. William F. Schulz. Philadelphia, PA: University of Pennsylvania Press, 2007, 30–33.

Freidson, Eliot. "Celebrating Ervin Goffman, 1983," (July 1983) *Contemporary Sociology*, 12:4, 359–362.

Frey, R. G. and Christopher W. Morris. "Violence, Terrorism, and Justice," in *Violence, Terrorism, and Justice*, eds R. G. Frey and Christopher W. Morris. Cambridge: Cambridge University Press, 1991, 1–17.

Gaita, Raimond. *Thinking About Torture*. Oxford and New York: Routledge, 2007.

Gaita, Raimond. "Torture: The Lesser Evil," (2006) *Tijdschrift-voor-Filosofie*, 68:2, 251–278.

Garcia, Antonia. "Prison of Women," in *The Phenomenon of Torture*, ed. William F. Schulz. Philadelphia, PA: University of Pennsylvania Press, 2007, 97–98.

Garro, Linda C. "Chronic Illnesses and the Construction of Narratives," in *Pain as Human Experience: An Anthropological Perspective*, eds Mary-Jo Delvecchio Good, Paul E. Brodwin, Byron J. Good, and Arthur Kleinman. Berkeley, CA: University of California Press, 1994, 100–137.

Gebert, Konstanty. "Black and White, or Gray: A Polish Conundrum," in *What Orwell Didn't Know: Propaganda and the New Face of American Politics*, ed. Szántó, András. New York: Public Affairs, 2007, 110–122.

Genefke, Inge. "Challenges for the Future," in *An End to Torture: Strategies for Its Eradication*, ed. Dunér, Bertil. New York: St. Martin's Press, 1999, 256–257.

Gerrity, Ellen, Terrence M. Keane, and Farris Tuma. *The Mental Health Consequences of Torture*. New York: Springer, 2001.

Gerrity, Ellen, Terrence M. Keane, Farris Tuma, and Sister Dianna Ortiz. "Future Directions," in *The Mental Health Consequences of Torture*, eds Ellen Gerrity, Terrence M. Keane, and Farris Tuma. New York: Springer, 2001, 335–342.

Gilbert, Paul. *New Terror, New Wars*. Washington, DC: Georgetown University Press, 2003.

Gildner, R. Matthew. "Psychological Torture as a Cold War Imperative," in *The Trauma of Psychological Torture,* ed. Almerindo E. Ojeda. Westport, CT: Praeger, 2008, 23–39.

Gillers, Stephen. "Legal Ethics: A Debate," in *The Torture Debate in America*, ed. Karen J. Greenberg. New York: Cambridge University Press, 2006, 236–240.

Glover, Jonathan. "State Terrorism," in *Violence, Terrorism, and Justice*, eds R. G. Frey and Christopher W. Morris. Cambridge: Cambridge University Press, 1991, 256–275.

Glucklich, Ariel. *Sacred Pain: Hurting the Body for the Sake of the Soul*. New York: Oxford University Press, 2001.

Goffman, Erving. *Asylums: Essays on the Social Situation of Mental Patients and Other Inmates*. New York: Aldine Transactions, 2007.

Goffman, Erving. *Frame Analysis: An Essay on the Organization of Experience*. New York: Harper and Row, 1974.

Goffman, Erving. *Gender Advertisements*. Cambridge, MA: Harvard University Press, 1979.

Goffman, Erving. *Interaction Ritual: Essays in Face-to-face Behavior*. New York: Pantheon, 1982.

Goffman, Erving. "The Nature of Deference and Demeanor," (1956) *American Anthropologist*, 58: 473–502.

Goffman, Erving. *The Presentation of Self in Everyday Life*. New York: Anchor, 1959.

Golden, Tim. "In U.S. Report, Brutal Details of 2 Afghan Inmates' Deaths," (2005) *The New York Times,* May 20, A1.

Golston, Joan C. "Ritual Abuse," in *The Phenomenon of Torture*, ed. William F. Schulz. Philadelphia, PA: University of Pennsylvania Press, 2007, 124–126.

Good, Byron J. "A Body In Pain—The Making of a World of Chronic Pain," in *Pain as Human Experience: An Anthropological Perspective*, eds Mary-Jo Delvecchio Good, Paul E. Brodwin, Byron J. Good, and Arthur Kleinman. Berkeley, CA: University of California Press, 1994, 29–48.

Gordon, Malcolm. "Domestic Violence in Families Exposed to Torture and Related Violence and Trauma," in *The Mental Health Consequences of Torture*, eds Ellen Gerrity, Terrence M. Keane, and Farris Tuma. New York: Springer, 2001, 227–248.

Graessner, Sepp. "Two Hundred Blows to the Head: Possibilities and Limits in Evaluating the Physical Aftereffects of Torture," in *At the Side of Torture Survivors: Treating a Terrible Assault on Human Dignity*, eds Sep Graessner, M. D., Norbert Gurris, and Christian Pross, M. D. Baltimore, MD: Johns Hopkins University Press, 2001, 153–168.

Graessner, Sepp, Salah Ahmad, and Frank Merkord. "Everything Forgotten! Memory Disorders among Refugees Who Have Been Tortured," in *At the Side of Torture Survivors: Treating a Terrible Assault on Human Dignity*, eds Sep Graessner, M. D., Norbert Gurris, and Christian Pross, M. D. Baltimore, MD: Johns Hopkins University Press, 2001, 184–197.

Grassian, Stuart. "Neuropsychic Effects of Solitary Confinement," in *The Trauma of Psychological Torture,* ed. Almerindo E. Ojeda. Westport, CT: Praeger, 2008, 113–126.

Gray, John. "Power and Vainglory," in *Abu Ghraib: The Politics of Torture*, ed. Anonymously with support of the Society for the Study of Native Arts and Sciences. Berkeley, CA: North Atlantic Books, 2004, 47–55.

Greenberg, Karen J. *The Torture Papers: The Road to Abu Ghraib.* Cambridge and New York: Cambridge University Press, 2005.

Gross, Oren. "The Prohibition on Torture and the Limits of the Law," in *Torture: A Collection*, ed. Sanford Levinson. New York: Oxford University Press, 2004, 229–256.

Grossinger, Richard. "Abu Ghraib: A Howl," in *Abu Ghraib: The Politics of Torture.* ed. Anonymously with support of the Society for the Study of Native Arts and Sciences. Berkeley, CA: North Atlantic Books, 2004, 123–140.

Gur-Arye, Miriam. "Can the War against Terror Justify the Use of Force in Interrogations? Reflections in Light of the Israeli Experience," in *Torture: A Collection*, ed. Sanford Levinson. New York: Oxford University Press, 2004, 183–198.

Gurris, Norbert. "Psychic Trauma through Torture—Healing through Psychotherapy?" in *At the Side of Torture Survivors: Treating a Terrible Assault on Human Dignity*, eds Sep Graessner, M. D., Norbert Gurris, and Christian Pross, M. D. Baltimore, MD: Johns Hopkins University Press, 2001, 29–56.

Gutierrez, Gitanjali S. Esq. "The Case of Mohammad al Qahtani," in *The Trauma of Psychological Torture,* ed. Almerindo E. Ojeda. Westport, CT: Praeger, 2008, 189–204.

Habermas, Jurgen. *Theory of Communicative Action Vol.2.* Boston, MA: Beacon Press, 1984.

Haenel, Ferdinand. "Foreign Bodies in the Soul," in *At the Side of Torture Survivors: Treating a Terrible Assault on Human Dignity*, eds Sep Graessner, M. D., Norbert Gurris, and Christian Pross, M. D. Baltimore, MD: Johns Hopkins University Press, 2001, 1–28.

Harbury, Jennifer K. *Truth, Torture, and the American Way: The History and Consequences of U.S. Involvement in Torture.* Boston, MA: Beacon Press, 2005.

Harding, Susan. "After the Falwellians," in *What Orwell Didn't Know: Propaganda and the New Face of American Politics*, ed. Szántó, András. New York: Public Affairs, 2007, 122–136.

Haritos-Fatouros, Mika. "The Official Torturer," in *The Phenomenon of Torture*, ed. William F. Schulz. Philadelphia, PA: University of Pennsylvania Press, 2007, 120–123.

Harris, David A. "Racial Profiling Revisited: 'Just Common Sense' in the Fight against Terror?" in *Civil Liberties vs. National Security in a Post-9/11 World*, eds M. Darmer, B. Katherine, Robert M. Baird, and Stuart E. Rosenbaum. Amherst, NY: Prometheus Books, 2004, 163–174.

Hathaway, Oona A. "The Promise and Limits of the International Law of Torture," in *Torture: A Collection*, ed. Sanford Levinson. New York: Oxford University Press, 2004, 199–212.

Hayner, Priscilla B. "The Contribution of Truth Commissions," in *An End to Torture: Strategies for Its Eradication*, ed. Dunér, Bertil. New York: St. Martin's Press, 1999, 203–221.

Hayner, Priscilla B. "The Contribution of Truth Commissions," in *The Phenomenon of Torture*, ed. William F. Schulz. Philadelphia, PA: University of Pennsylvania Press, 2007, 333–346.

Held, Virginia. "Terrorism, rights, and political goals," in *Violence, Terrorism, and Justice*, eds R. G. Frey and Christopher W. Morris. Cambridge: Cambridge University Press, 1991, 59–85.

Hentoff, Nat. "No President is Above the US Constitution," in *Civil Liberties vs. National Security in a Post-9/11 World*, eds M. Darmer, B. Katherine, Robert M. Baird, and Stuart E. Rosenbaum. Amherst, NY: Prometheus Books, 2004, 295–298.

Heymann, Philip B. "Torture Should Not Be Authorized," in *Civil Liberties vs. National Security in a Post-9/11 World*, eds M. Darmer, B. Katherine, Robert M. Baird, and Stuart E. Rosenbaum. Amherst, NY: Prometheus Books, 2004, 215–218.

Hill, Thomas E. Jr. "Making Exceptions Without Abandoning the Principle: or How a Kantian Might Think About Terrorism," in *Violence, Terrorism, and Justice*, eds R. G. Frey and Christopher W. Morris. Cambridge: Cambridge University Press, 1991, 196–229.

Himma, Kenneth Einar. "Assessing the Prohibition Against Torture," in *Intervention, Terrorism and Torture: Contemporary Challenges to Just War Theory*, ed. Steven P. Lee. The Netherlands: Springer Publication, 2006, 235–248.

Hochschild, Adam. "The Torturer's Notebooks," in *The Phenomenon of Torture*, ed. William F. Schulz. Philadelphia, PA: University of Pennsylvania Press, 2007, 136.

Holmes, Stephen. "Is Defiance of Law a Proof of Success? Magical Thinking in the War on Terror," in *The Torture Debate in America*, ed. Karen J. Greenberg. New York: Cambridge University Press, 2006, 118–135.

Holmström, Lee (ed.). *Conclusions and Recommendations of the UN Committee against Torture.* The Hague: Martinus Nijhoff Publishers, 2000.

Horton, Scott. "Through a Mirror, Darkly: Applying the Geneva Conventions to 'A New Kind of Warfare'," in *The Torture Debate in America*, ed. Karen J. Greenberg. New York: Cambridge University Press, 2006, 136–150.

Huggins, Martha K., Mika Haritos-Fatouros, and Philip G. Zimbardo. *Violence Workers: Police Torturers and Murderers Reconstruct Brazilian Atrocities.* Berkeley and Los Angeles, CA: University of California Press, 2002.

Ignatieff, Michael. "Moral Prohibition at a Price," in *Torture: Does it Make Us Safer? Is It Ever OK? A Human Rights Perspective*, eds Kenneth Roth and Minky Worden. New York: The New Press and Human Rights Watch, 2005, 18–27.

Ignatieff, Michael. *The Lesser Evil: Political Ethics in an Age of Terror*. Princeton, NJ: Princeton University Press, 2004.

Jackson, Jean E. "'After a While No One Believes You': Real and Unreal Pain," in *Pain as Human Experience: An Anthropological Perspective*, eds Mary-Jo Delvecchio Good, Paul E. Brodwin, Byron J. Good, and Arthur Kleinman. Berkeley, CA: University of California Press, 1994 138–168.

Jacobs, Uwe. "Documenting the Neurobiology of Psychological Torture: Conceptual and Neuropsychological Observations," in *The Trauma of Psychological Torture*, ed. Almerindo E. Ojeda. Westport, CT: Praeger, 2008, 163–172.

Jacobsen, Lone and Edith Montgomery. "Treatment of Victims of Torture," in *An End to Torture: Strategies for Its Eradication*, ed. Dunér, Bertil. New York: St. Martin's Press, 1999, 133–153.

Jacobsen, Lone and Edith Montgomery. "Treatment of Victims of Torture," in *The Phenomenon of Torture*, ed. William F. Schulz. Philadelphia, PA: University of Pennsylvania Press, 2007, 285–296.

Jaffer, Jameel, and Amrit Singh. *Administration of Torture: A Documentary Record from Washington to Abu Ghraib and Beyond*. Irvington, NY: Columbia University Press, 2007.

Jaranson, James M. and Michael K. Popkin. *Caring for Victims of Torture*. New York: American Psychiatric Publishing, Inc., 1998.

Jaranson, James M., Kinzie, David J., Friedman, Merle, Sister Ortiz, Dianna, Friedman, Matthew J., Southwick, Steven, Kastrup, Marianne, and Mollica, Richard. "Assessment, Diagnosis, and Intervention," in *The Mental Health Consequences of Torture*, eds Ellen Gerrity, Terrence M. Keane, and Farris Tuma. New York: Springer, 2001, 249–276.

Jenkins, Britta. "There, Where Words Fail, Tears are the Bridge: Thoughts on Speechlessness in Working With Survivors of Torture," in *At the Side of Torture Survivors: Treating a Terrible Assault on Human Dignity*, eds Sep Graessner, M. D., Norbert Gurris, and Christian Pross, M. D. Baltimore, MD: Johns Hopkins University Press, 2001, 142–152.

Kahana, Boaz and Eva Kahana. "Holocaust Trauma and Sequelae," in *The Mental Health Consequences of Torture*, eds Ellen Gerrity, Terrence M. Keane, and Farris Tuma. New York: Springer, 2001, 143–158.

Kant, Immanuel. *Critique of Practical Reason*, ed./trans. Mary Gregor. Cambridge: Cambridge University Press, 1997.

Kant, Immanuel. *Groundwork for the Metaphysics of Morals*, ed./trans. Mary Gregor. Cambridge: Cambridge University Press, 1997.

Kaplan, Martin. "Welcome to the Information Freak Show," in *What Orwell Didn't Know: Propaganda and the New Face of American Politics*, ed. Szántó, András. New York: Public Affairs, 2007, 137–146.

Karcher, Sylvia. "'In My Fingertips I Don't Have a Soul Anymore': Body Psychotherapy with Survivors of Torture—Insights into Work with Concentrative Movement Therapy," in *At the Side of Torture Survivors: Treating a Terrible Assault on Human Dignity*, eds Sep Graessner, M. D., Norbert Gurris, and Christian Pross, M. D. Baltimore, MD: Johns Hopkins University Press, 2001, 70–94.

Kavka, Gregory S. "Nuclear Hostages," in *Violence, Terrorism, and Justice*, eds R. G. Frey and Christopher W. Morris. Cambridge: Cambridge University Press, 1991, 276–298.

Kellberg, Love. "Torture: International Rules and Procedures," in *An End to Torture: Strategies for Its Eradication*, ed. Dunér, Bertil. St. Martin's Press, 1999, 3–38.

Kerrigan, Michael. *The Instruments of Torture*. Guilford, DE: The Lyons Press, 2007.

Kershnar, Stephen. "For Interrogational Torture," (2005) *International Journal of Applied Philosophy*, 19:2, 223–241.

Kershnar, Stephen. "Objections to the Systematic Imposition of Punitive Torture," (1999) *International Journal of Applied Philosophy*, 13:1, 47–56.

Kilpatrick, Dean G. and Margaret E. Ross. "Torture and Human Rights Violations: Public Policy and the Law," in *The Mental Health Consequences of Torture*, eds Ellen Gerrity, Terrence M. Keane, and Farris Tuma. New York: Springer, 2001, 317–334.

Kilpatrick, Dean G. and Mary P. Koss. "Homicide and Physical Assault," in *The Mental Health Consequences of Torture*, eds Ellen Gerrity, Terrence M. Keane, and Farris Tuma. New York: Springer, 2001, 195–210.

Kinzie, J. David and Brian Engdahl. "Professional Caregiver and Observer Issues," in *The Mental Health Consequences of Torture*, eds Ellen Gerrity, Terrence M. Keane, and Farris Tuma. New York: Springer, 2001, 309–316.

Kinzie, J. David and James M. Jaranson. "Refugees and Asylum-Seekers," in *The Mental Health Consequences of Torture*, eds Ellen Gerrity, Terrence M. Keane, and Farris Tuma. New York: Springer, 2001, 111–120.

Klayman, B. M. "The Definition of Torture in International Law," (1978) *Temple Law Quarterly*, 51, 449–517.

Kleinman, Arthur. "Pain and Resistance: The Delegitimation and Relegitimation of Local Worlds," in *Pain as Human Experience: An Anthropological Perspective*, eds Mary-Jo Delvecchio Good, Paul E. Brodwin, Byron J. Good, and Arthur Kleinman. Berkeley, CA: University of California Press, 1994, 169–197.

Kleinman, Arthur, Paul E. Brodwin, Byron J. Good, and Mary-Jo Delvecchio Good. "Pain as Human Experience: An Introduction," in *Pain as Human Experience: An Anthropological Perspective*, eds Mary-Jo Delvecchio Good, Paul E. Brodwin, Byron J. Good, and Arthur Kleinman. Berkeley, CA: University of California Press, 1994, 1–28.

Kois, Lisa M. "Dance, Sister, Dance!" in *An End to Torture: Strategies for Its Eradication*, ed. Dunér, Bertil. St. Martin's Press, 1998, 85–109.

Korovessis, Pericles. "The Method," in *The Phenomenon of Torture*, ed. William F. Schulz. Philadelphia, PA: University of Pennsylvania Press, 2007, 71–79.

Korovessis, Pericles. *The Method: A Personal Account of the Tortures in Greece* Trans. by Les Nightingale and Catherine Patrakis, London: Panther, 1970.

Koss, Mary P. and Dean G. Kilpatrick. "Rape and Sexual Assault," in *The Mental Health Consequences of Torture*, eds Ellen Gerrity, Terrence M. Keane, and Farris Tuma. New York: Springer, 2001, 177–195.

Krauthammer, Charles. "The Truth About Torture," in *Torture: A Collection*, ed. Sanford Levinson. New York: Oxford University Press, 2004, 307–316.

Kupers, Terry A. "Prison and the Decimation of Pro-Social Life Skills," in *The Trauma of Psychological Torture,* ed. Almerindo E. Ojeda. Westport, CT: Praeger, 2008, 127–138.

Kutz, Christopher. "The Lawyers Know Sin," in *The Torture Debate in America*, ed. Karen J. Greenberg. New York: Cambridge University Press, 2006, 241–246.

Lakoff, George. "What Orwell Didn't Know About the Brain, the Mind, and Language," in *What Orwell Didn't Know: Propaganda and the New Face of American Politics*, ed. Szántó, András. New York: Public Affairs, 2007, 67–75.

Langbein, John H. "The Legal History of Torture," in *Torture: A Collection*, ed. Sanford Levinson. New York: Oxford University Press, 2004, 93–104.

Langbein, John H. *Torture and the Law of Proof: Europe and England in the Ancient Regime*. Chicago, IL: University Of Chicago Press, 2006.

Langbein, John H. "Torture and the Law of Truth," in *The Phenomenon of Torture*, ed. William F. Schulz. Philadelphia, PA: University of Pennsylvania Press, 2007, 19–26.

Langguth, A. J. "Hidden Terrors," in *The Phenomenon of Torture*, ed. William F. Schulz. Philadelphia, PA: University of Pennsylvania Press, 2007, 127–131.

Lansen, Johan. "What Does This Work Do to Us?" in *At the Side of Torture Survivors: Treating a Terrible Assault on Human Dignity*, eds Sep Graessner, M. D., Norbert Gurris, and Christian Pross, M. D. Baltimore, MD: Johns Hopkins University Press, 2001, 198–211.

Lazreg, Marnia. *Torture and the Twilight of Empire*. Princeton, NJ: Princeton University Press, 2008.

Lee Meyes, Steven and Mark Mazzetti, "Bush Vetoes a Bill on CIA Tactics, Affirms Legacy," (March 9, 2008) *New York Times,* A1.

Lemann, Nicholas. "The Limits of Language," in *What Orwell Didn't Know: Propaganda and the New Face of American Politics*, ed. Szántó, András. New York: Public Affairs, 2007, 9–15.

Lemert, Edwin. *Human Deviance, Social Problems, and Social Control*, Prentice-Hall, Upper Saddle River, NJ, 1972, 18.

Lenta, Patrick. "The Purposes of Torture," (2006) *South African Journal of Philosophy*, 25:1, 48–61.

Levi, Primo. *Survival in Auschwitz*. New York: Touchstone, 1958.

Levin, Michael. "The Case for Torture," in *The Phenomenon of Torture*, ed. William F. Schulz. Philadelphia, PA: University of Pennsylvania Press, 2007, 227–229.

Levinas, Emmanuel. *Totality and Infinity*. Trans. Alphonso Lingis. Pittsburgh, PA: Duquesne University Press, 1969.

Lifton, Robert Jay. *The Nazi Doctors: Medical Killing and the Psychology of Genocide*. New York: Basic Books, 1986.

Lincoln, Bruce. *Religion, Empire, and Torture: The Case of Achaemenian Persia, with a Postscript on Abu Ghraib*. Chicago, IL: University Of Chicago Press, 2007.

Lingis, Alphonso F. *The Community of Those Who Have Nothing in Common*, Bloomington and Indianapolis, IN: Indiana University Press, 1994.

Lomasky, Loren E. "The Political Significance of Terrorism," in *Violence, Terrorism, and Justice*, eds R. G. Frey and Christopher W. Morris. Cambridge: Cambridge University Press, 1991, 86–116.

Lomax, Eric. "The Railway Man," in *The Phenomenon of Torture*, ed. William F. Schulz. Philadelphia, PA: University of Pennsylvania Press, 2007, 49–52.

Luban, David. "Liberalism, Torture, and the Ticking Bomb," in *The Torture Debate in America*, ed. Karen J. Greenberg. New York: Cambridge University Press, 2006, 35–83.

Luban, David. "The War on Terrorism and the End of Human Rights," (2002) *Philosophy and Public Policy Quarterly,* 22:3, 9–14.

MacDonald, Heather. "How to Interrogate Terrorists," in *The Torture Debate in America,* ed. Karen J. Greenberg. New York: Cambridge University Press, 2006, 84–97.

Machan, Tibor R. "Exploring Extreme Violence (Torture)," (Spring 1990) *Journal of Social Philosophy*, 21, 92–97.

Mackey, Chris and Greg Miller. *The Interrogators: Inside the Secret War Against Al Qaeda*. New York: Back Bay Books, 2004.

MacMahan, Jeff. *The Ethics of Killing: Problems at the Margins of Life*. New York: Oxford University Press, 2002.

Magruder, Kathryn M., Richard Mollica, and Merle Friedman. "Mental Health Services Research: Implications for Survivors of Torture," in *The Mental Health Consequences of Torture*, eds Ellen Gerrity, Terrence M. Keane, and Farris Tuma. New York: Springer, 2001, 291–308.

Makiya, Kanan. "Republic of Fear," in *The Phenomenon of Torture*, ed. William F. Schulz. Philadelphia, PA: University of Pennsylvania Press, 2007, 201–203.

Malinowski, Tom. "Banned State Department Practices," in *Torture: Does it Make Us Safer? Is It Ever OK? A Human Rights Perspective*, eds Kenneth Roth and Minky Worden. New York: The New Press and Human Rights Watch, 2005, 139–144.

Malpas, Jeff and Norelle Lickiss (eds) *Perspectives on Human Dignity: A Conversation*, Dordrecht, the Netherlands: Springer, 2007.

Mannix, Daniel P. *The History of Torture*. Phoenix Mill: Sutton Publishing, 2003.

Maran, Rita. "The Role of Non-governmental Organizations," in *An End to Torture: Strategies for Its Eradication*, ed. Dunér, Bertil. New York: St. Martin's Press, 1999, 222–246.

Marks, Jonathan H. "Doctors as Pawns? Law and Medical Ethics at Guantanamo Bay," in *The Trauma of Psychological Torture,* ed. Almerindo E. Ojeda. Westport, CT: Praeger, 2008, 92–113.

Marsella, Anthony J. "Measurement Issues," in *The Mental Health Consequences of Torture*, ed. Ellen Gerrity, Terrence M. Keane, and Farris Tuma. New York: Springer, 2001, 277–290.

Martindale, Don. *The Nature and Types of Sociological Theory.* New York: Houghton Mifflin, 1981, 364.

Massing, Michael. "Our Own Thought Police," in *What Orwell Didn't Know: Propaganda and the New Face of American Politics*, ed. Szántó, András. New York: Public Affairs, 2007, 174–186.

Matlin, David. "Abu Ghraib: The Surround," in *Abu Ghraib: The Politics of Torture*. ed. Anonymously with support of the Society for the Study of Native Arts and Sciences. Berkeley, CA: North Atlantic Books, 2004, 60–64.

Matthews, Daryl. "The Case of Salim Hamdan (Declaration of Daryl Matthews)," in *The Trauma of Psychological Torture,* ed. Almerindo E. Ojeda. Westport, CT: Praeger, 2008, 205–208.

May, Larry. "Torturing Detainees During Interrogation," (2005) *International Journal of Applied Philosophy*, 19:2, 193–208.

May, Larry. *War Crimes and Just War*. Cambridge: Cambridge University Press, 2007.

Mayer, Jane. *The Dark Side.* New York: Doubleday, 2008.

McCabe, Joseph. *The History Of Torture: A Study Of Cruelty, The Ugliest Impulse In Man*. Whitefish, MT: Kessinger Publishing, LLC, 2007.

McCain, John. "Respecting the Geneva Conventions," in *Torture: Does it Make Us Safer? Is It Ever OK? A Human Rights Perspective*, eds Kenneth Roth and Minky Worden. New York: The New Press and Human Rights Watch, 2005, 155–157.

McCarthy, Andrew C. "Torture: Thinking About the Unthinkable," in *The Torture Debate in America*, ed. Karen J. Greenberg. New York: Cambridge University Press, 2006, 98–110.

McCauley, Clark. "Toward a Social Psychology of Professional Military Interrogation," (November 2007) *Peace and Conflict: Journal of Peace Psychology*, 13:4, 399–410.

McCoy, Alfred W. "Legacy of a Dark Decade: CIA Mind Control, Classified Behavioral Research, and the Origins of Modern Medical Ethics," in *The Trauma of Psychological Torture,* ed. Almerindo E. Ojeda. Westport, CT: Praeger, 2008, 40–69.

McCoy, Alfred W. *A Question of Torture: CIA Interrogation, from the Cold War to the War on Terror*. New York: Owl Books, 2006.

McKelvey, Tara. *Monstering: Inside America's Policy of Secret Interrogations and Torture in the Terror War*. New York: Carroll & Graf, 2007.

Mendez, Juan E. "Torture in Latin America," in *Torture: Does it Make Us Safer? Is It Ever OK? A Human Rights Perspective*, eds Kenneth Roth and Minky Worden. New York: The New Press and Human Rights Watch, 2005, 55–68.

Merkord, Frank. "'Like a Drop of Water': Everyday Life for Asylum Seekers and Social Work with Survivors of Torture," in *At the Side of Torture Survivors: Treating a Terrible Assault on Human Dignity*, eds Sep Graessner, M. D., Norbert Gurris, and Christian Pross, M. D. Baltimore, MD: Johns Hopkins University Press, 2001, 169–183.

Miles, Steven H. *Oath Betrayed: Torture, Medical Complicity, and the War on Terror*. New York: Random House, 2006.

Milgram, Stanley. *Obedience to Authority*. New York: HarperPerennial, 1974.

Milgram, Stanley. "The Perils of Obedience," in *The Phenomenon of Torture*, ed. William F. Schulz. Philadelphia, PA: University of Pennsylvania Press, 2007, 110–119.

Miller, Arthur G. "What Can the Milgram Obedience Experiments Tell Us about the Holocaust?: Generalizing from the Social Psychology Laboratory," in *The Social Psychology of Good and Evil*, ed. Arthur G. Miller. New York: The Guilford Press, 2005, 193–239.

Miller, Seumas. "Is Torture Ever Morally Justifiable?" (2005) *International Journal of Applied Philosophy*, 19:2, 179–192.

Miller, Seumas. "Torture and Counterterrorism," (2006) *Iyyun*, 25:1, 62–76.

Millet, Kate. "The Politics of Cruelty," in *The Phenomenon of Torture*, ed. William F. Schulz. Philadelphia, PA: University of Pennsylvania Press, 2007, 163–166.

Mitchell, Andrew J. "Torture and Photography: Abu Ghraib," (2005) *The Philosopher's Index*, 8:1, 1–27.

Mora, Alberto J. "Memorandum from Navy General Counsel Alberto J. Mora to Navy Inspector General, July 7, 2004." *American Civil Liberties Union*. Published by the *New Yorker*, February 2006. 2007–2008. http://www.aclu.org/pdfs/safefree/mora_memo_july_2004.pdf

Moran, Sherwood F. "Suggestions for Japanese Interpreters," in *The Phenomenon of Torture*, ed. William F. Schulz. Philadelphia, PA: University of Pennsylvania Press, 2007, 249–254.

Muehlenhard, Charlene L. and Zoe D. Peterson. "Conceptualizing Sexual Violence: Socially Acceptable Coercion and Other Controversies," in *The Social Psychology of Good and Evil*, ed. Arthur G. Miller. New York: The Guilford Press, 2005, 240–268.

Narveson, Jan. "Terrorism and Morality," in *Violence, Terrorism, and Justice*, eds R. G. Frey and Christopher W. Morris. Cambridge: Cambridge University Press, 1991, 116–169.

Nathanson, Stephen. "Terrorism, Supreme Emergency, Noncombatant Immunity: A Critique of Michael Walzer's Ethics of War," (2006) *The Jerusalem Philosophical Quarterly*, 55, 3–26.

Navasky, Victor. "Neither Snow, Nor Rain, Nor Heat, Nor Gloom of Night Will Stay the Couriers from the Swift Completion of Their Appointed Rounds—but What About Big Media?" in *What Orwell Didn't Know: Propaganda and the New Face of American Politics*, ed. Szántó, András. New York: Public Affairs, 2007, 147–157.

Neier, Aryeh. "Freedom, Liberty, and Rights: Three Cautionary Tales," in *What Orwell Didn't Know: Propaganda and the New Face of American Politics*, ed. Szántó, András. New York: Public Affairs, 2007, 49–56.

Neier, Aryeh. "Lost Liberties: Ashcroft and the Assault on Personal Freedom," in *Civil Liberties vs. National Security in a Post-9/11 World*, eds M. Darmer, B. Katherine, Robert M. Baird, and Stuart E. Rosenbaum. Amherst, NY: Prometheus Books, 2004, 31–42.

Nietzsche, Friedrich Wilhelm. *Human, All Too Human: A Book for Free Spirits.* Lincoln, NE: University of Nebraska Press, 1996.

Nowak, Manfred. "On the Prevention of Torture," in *An End to Torture: Strategies for Its Eradication*, ed. Dunér, Bertil. St. Martin's Press, 1999, 247–251.

O'Connor, Alice. "Bad Knowledge," in *What Orwell Didn't Know: Propaganda and the New Face of American Politics*, ed. Szántó, András. New York: Public Affairs, 2007, 97–109.

O'Neill, Onora. "What are the Offers *You* can't Refuse?" in *Violence, Terrorism, and Justice*, eds R. G. Frey and Christopher W. Morris. Cambridge: Cambridge University Press, 1991, 170–195.

Ojeda, Almerindo E. *The Trauma of Psychological Torture.* Westport, CT: Praeger, 2008.

Ojeda, Almerindo E. "What is Psychological Torture?" in *The Trauma of Psychological Torture,* ed. Almerindo E. Ojeda. Westport, CT: Praeger, 2008, 1–22.

Ortiz, Sister Dianna. "The Survivors' Perspective: Voices from the Center," in *The Mental Health Consequences of Torture*, eds Ellen Gerrity, Terrence M. Keane, and Farris Tuma. New York: Springer, 2001, 13–34.

Orwell, George. *Nineteen Eighty-Four.* London: Plume, 1984.

Orwell, George. "Politics and the English Language," in *What Orwell Didn't Know: Propaganda and the New Face of American Politics*, ed. Szántó, András. New York: Public Affairs, 2007, 205–222.

Osiel, Mark. "The Mental State of Torturers: Argentina's Dirty War," in *Torture: A Collection*, ed. Sanford Levinson. New York: Oxford University Press, 2004, 129–144.

Otterman, Michael. *American Torture: From the Cold War to Abu Ghraib and Beyond.* London: Pluto Press, 2007.

Outhwaite, William. *Habermas: A Critical Introduction.* Stanford, CA: Stanford University Press, 1994.

Paden, Roger. "Surveillance and Torture: Foucault and Orwell on the Methods of Discipline," (1984) *Social Theory and Practice*, 10:3, 261–271.

Parenti, Christian. "Fear as Institution: 9/11 and Surveillance Triumphant," in *Civil Liberties vs. National Security in a Post-9/11 World*, eds M. Darmer, B. Katherine., Robert M. Baird, and and Stuart E. Rosenbaum. Amherst, NY: Prometheus Books, 2004, 115–134.

Parry, John T. "Escalation and Necessity: Defining Torture at Home and Abroad," in *Torture: A Collection*, ed. Sanford Levinson. New York: Oxford University Press, 2004, 145–164.

Parry, John T. and Welsh S. White. "Interrogating Suspected Terrorists: Should Torture Be an Option?" (2002) *The University of Pittsburgh Law Review*, 63, 743–766.

Pearlstein, Deborah. "Reconciling Torture With Democracy," in *The Torture Debate in America*, ed. Karen J. Greenberg. New York: Cambridge University Press, 2006, 253–255.

Pennegård, Ann-Marie Bolin. "An Optional Protocol, Based on Prevention and Cooperation," in *An End to Torture: Strategies for Its Eradication*, ed. Dunér, Bertil. New York: St. Martin's Press, 1999, 39–62.

Perry, John. *Torture: Religious Ethics and National Security*. Maryknoll: Orbis Books, 2005.

Peters, Edward. *Torture*. Philadelphia, PA: University of Pennsylvania Press, 1985.

Pheto, Molefe. "And Night Fell," in *The Phenomenon of Torture*, ed. William F. Schulz. Philadelphia, PA: University of Pennsylvania Press, 2007, 53–59.

Pohlman, H. L. *Terrorism and the Constitution: The Post-9/11 Cases.* New York: Rowman and Littlefield, 2008.

Pokempner, Dinah. "Command Responsibility for Torture," in *Torture: Does it Make Us Safer? Is It Ever OK? A Human Rights Perspective*, eds Kenneth Roth and Minky Worden. New York: The New Press and Human Rights Watch, 2005, 158–172.

Posner, Richard. "Torture, Terrorism, and Interrogation," in *Torture: A Collection*, ed. Sanford Levinson. New York: Oxford University Press, 2004, 291–298.

Press, Eyal. "In Torture We Trust?" in *Civil Liberties vs. National Security in a Post-9/11 World*, eds M. Darmer, B. Katherine, Robert M. Baird, and Stuart E. Rosenbaum. Amherst, NY: Prometheus Books, 2004, 219–228.

Prose, Francine. "Sloppiness and the English Language," in *What Orwell Didn't Know: Propaganda and the New Face of American Politics*, ed. Szántó, András. New York: Public Affairs, 2007, 57–66.

Pross, Christian. "'Every Perpetrator's Acquittal Costs Me Two Weeks' Sleep': How Societies and Individuals Cope With Trauma, as Illustrated by the German Democratic Republic," in *At the Side of Torture Survivors: Treating a Terrible Assault on Human Dignity*, eds Sep Graessner, M. D., Norbert Gurris, and Christian Pross, M. D. Baltimore, MD: Johns Hopkins University Press, 2001, 126–141.

Pross, Christian. "Legal Status, Living Conditions, and Health Care for Political Refugees in Germany," in *At the Side of Torture Survivors:*

Treating a Terrible Assault on Human Dignity, eds Sep Graessner, M. D., Norbert Gurris, and Christian Pross, M. D. Baltimore, MD: Johns Hopkins University Press, 2001, 212–218.

Pynoos, Robert S, J. David Kinzie, and Malcolm Gordon. "Children, Adolescents, and Families Exposed to Torture and Related Trauma," in *The Mental Health Consequences of Torture*, eds Ellen Gerrity, Terrence M. Keane, and Farris Tuma. New York: Springer, 2001, 211–226.

Quiroga, J. and Jaranson, J. M. "Politically-Motivated Torture and its Survivors: A Desk Study Review of the Literature," (2005) *Torture*, 15: (2–3), 39–45.

Ratner, Michael and Peter Weiss. "Litigating Against Torture: The German Criminal Prosecution," in *The Torture Debate in America*, ed. Karen J. Greenberg. New York: Cambridge University Press, 2006, 261–266.

Rehnquist, William. "Inter Arma Silent Leges," in *Civil Liberties vs. National Security in a Post-9/11 World*, eds M. Darmer, B. Katherine, Robert M. Baird, and Stuart E. Rosenbaum. Amherst, NY: Prometheus Books, 2004, 23–30.

Reisman, W. Michael and Chris T. Anoniou (eds) *The Laws of War: A Comprehensive Collection of Primary Documents on International Laws Governing Armed Conflict.* New York: Vintage Books, 1994.

Rejali, Darius M. "Does Torture Work?" in *The Phenomenon of Torture*, ed. William F. Schulz. Philadelphia, PA: University of Pennsylvania Press, 2007, 255–259.

Rejali, Darius M. *Torture and Democracy*, Princeton, NJ: Princeton University Press, 2007.

Rejali, Darius M. *Torture and Modernity: Self, Society, and State in Modern Iran.* Boulder, CO: Westview Press, 1984.

Resolution of Advice and Consent to Ratification of the Convention Against Torture and Other Forms of Cruel, Inhuman or Degrading Treatment or Punishment: Reservations, Declarations, and Understandings, part II (1)(a), 136 Cong. Rec S17491 (daily edition, October 27, 1990).

Rieff, David. "Orwell Then and Now," in *What Orwell Didn't Know: Propaganda and the New Face of American Politics*, ed. Szántó, András. New York: Public Affairs, 2007, 3–8.

Roberts, Adam and Richard Guelff. *Documents on the Laws of War.* Oxford: Clarendon Press, 1989.

Robertson, Geoffrey. "An End to Impunity," in *The Phenomenon of Torture*, ed. William F. Schulz. Philadelphia, PA: University of Pennsylvania Press, 2007, 311–313.

Robertson, Geoffrey. "The Case of General Pinochet," in *The Phenomenon of Torture*, ed. William F. Schulz. Philadelphia, PA: University of Pennsylvania Press, 2007, 4–324.

Robin, Marie-Monique. "Counterinsurgency and Torture: Exporting Torture Tactics from Indochina and Algeria to Latin America," in *Torture: Does it Make Us Safer? Is It Ever OK? A Human Rights*

Perspective, eds Kenneth Roth and Minky Worden. New York: The New Press and Human Rights Watch, 2005, 44–54.

Rodin, David. *War, Torture and Terrorism: Ethics and War in the 21st Century.* Oxford and Boston, MA: Blackwell Publishing Limited, 2007.

Rodley, Sir Nigel, interviewed by Amy D. Bernstein. "On Negotiating With Torturers," in *Torture: Does it Make Us Safer? Is It Ever OK? A Human Rights Perspective*, eds Kenneth Roth and Minky Worden. New York: The New Press and Human Rights Watch, 2005, 106–116.

Ross, James. "A History of Torture," in *Torture: Does it Make Us Safer? Is It Ever OK? A Human Rights Perspective*, eds Kenneth Roth and Minky Worden. New York: The New Press and Human Rights Watch, 2005, 3–17.

Roth, Kenneth. "Justifying Torture," in *Torture: Does it Make Us Safer? Is It Ever OK? A Human Rights Perspective*, eds Kenneth Roth and Minky Worden. New York: The New Press and Human Rights Watch, 2005, 184–201.

Rothkegel, Sibylle. "The Frozen Lake: Gestalt Dreamwork with Torture Victims," in *At the Side of Torture Survivors: Treating a Terrible Assault on Human Dignity*, eds Sep Graessner, M. D., Norbert Gurris, and Christian Pross, M. D. Baltimore, MD: Johns Hopkins University Press, 2001, 95–111.

Rubenstein, Richard L. "The Bureaucratization of Torture," (1982) *Journal of Social Philosophy*, 13: 31–51.

Rupp, Agnes and Eliot Sorel. "Economic Models," in *The Mental Health Consequences of Torture*, eds Ellen Gerrity, Terrence M. Keane, and Farris Tuma. New York: Springer, 2001, 89–110.

Ryan, Alan. "State and Private, Red and White," in *Violence, Terrorism, and Justice*, eds R. G. Frey and Christopher W. Morris. Cambridge: Cambridge University Press, 1991, 230–255.

Sands, Philippe. *Torture Team: Rumsfeld's Memo and the Betrayal of American Values.* New York: Palgrave Macmillan, 2008.

Scarry, Elaine. "Five Errors in the Reasoning of Alan Dershowitz," in *Torture: A Collection*, ed. Sanford Levinson. New York: Oxford University Press, 2004, 281–290.

Scarry, Elaine. *The Body in Pain: The Making and Unmaking of the World.* New York: Oxford University Press, 1985.

Schelling, Thomas C. "What Purposes can 'International Terrorism' Serve?" in *Violence, Terrorism, and Justice*, eds R. G. Frey and Christopher W. Morris. Cambridge: Cambridge University Press, 1991, 18–32.

Schulhofer, Stephen J. "No Checks, No Balances: Discarding Bedrock Constitutional Principles," in *Civil Liberties vs. National Security in a Post-9/11 World*, eds M. Darmer, B. Katherine, Robert M. Baird, and Stuart E. Rosenbaum. Amherst, NY: Prometheus Books, 2004, 23–30.

Schulz, William. "Tainted Legacy," in *The Phenomenon of Torture*, ed. William F. Schulz. Philadelphia, PA: University of Pennsylvania Press, 2007, 260–266.

Second Circuit Court of Appeals. *Padilla v. Rumsfeld,* in *Civil Liberties vs. National Security in a Post-9/11 World,* eds M. Darmer, B. Katherine, Robert M. Baird, and Stuart E. Rosenbaum. Amherst, NY: Prometheus Books, 2004, 263–294.

Shakespeare, William. *As You Like It.* New York: Washington Square Press, 2004.

Shapiro, Jeffrey K. "Legal Ethics and Other Perspectives," in *The Torture Debate in America,* ed. Karen J. Greenberg. New York: Cambridge University Press, 2006, 229–235.

Sherman, Nancy. "Torturers and the Tortured," (2006) *South African Journal of Philosophy,* 25:1, 77–88.

Shue, Henry. "Torture," in *Torture: A Collection,* ed. Sanford Levinson. New York: Oxford University Press, 2004, 47–60.

Silove, Derrick and J. David Kinzie. "Survivors of War Trauma, Mass Violence, and Civilian Terror," in *The Mental Health Consequences of Torture,* eds Ellen Gerrity, Terrence M. Keane, and Farris Tuma. New York: Springer, 2001, 159–176.

Singer, Peter. *The President of Good and Evil.* New York: Dutton, 2004.

Skolnick, Jerome H. "American Interrogation: From Torture to Trickery," in *Torture: A Collection,* ed. Sanford Levinson. New York: Oxford University Press, 2004, 105–129.

Smith, Christopher H. *U.S. Policy Towards Victims of Torture: Hearing Before the Committee on International Relations, U.S. House of Representatives.* Darby, PA: Diane Pub Co., 1999.

Smith, Greg. *Erving Goffman.* Routledge, 2006, 103.

Soldz, Stephen and Brad Olson, "Psychologists, Detainee Interrogations, and Torture: Varying Perspectives on Nonparticipation," in *The Trauma of Psychological Torture,* ed. Almerindo E. Ojeda. Westport, CT: Praeger, 2008, 70–91.

Solzhenitsyn, Aleksandr. "Statement by Abu Ghraib Detainee," in *The Phenomenon of Torture,* ed. William F. Schulz. Philadelphia, PA: University of Pennsylvania Press, 2007, 60–62.

Sontag, Susan. *Regarding the Pain of Others.* New York: Picador, 2003.

Sorenson, Bent. "Torture and Asylum," in *An End to Torture: Strategies for Its Eradication,* ed. Dunér, Bertil. St. Martin's Press, 1999, 172–182.

Soros, George. "Epilogue: What I Didn't Know: Open Society Reconsidered," in *What Orwell Didn't Know: Propaganda and the New Face of American Politics,* ed. Szántó, András. New York: Public Affairs, 2007, 187–204.

Soros, George. *The Age of Fallibility: Consequences of the War on Terror.* New York: Public Affairs, 2007.

Sottas, Eric. "Perpetrators of Torture," in *An End to Torture: Strategies for Its Eradication,* ed. Dunér, Bertil. New York: St. Martin's Press, 1999, 63–84.

Southwick, Steven and Matthew J. Friedman. "Neurobiological Models of Posttraumatic Stress Disorder," in *The Mental Health Consequences of Torture,* eds Ellen Gerrity, Terrence M. Keane, and Farris Tuma. New York: Springer, 2001, 73–88.

Stanley, Jay and Barry Steinhardt. "Bigger Monster, Weaker Chains: The Growth of an American Surveillance Society," in *Civil Liberties vs. National Security in a Post-9/11 World*, eds M. Darmer, B. Katherine, Robert M. Baird, and Stuart E. Rosenbaum. Amherst, NY: Prometheus Books, 2004, 53–80.

Stein, Charles. "Abu Ghraib and the Magic of Images," in *Abu Ghraib: The Politics of Torture*, ed. Anonymously with support of the Society for the Study of Native Arts and Sciences. Berkeley, CA: North Atlantic Books, 2004, 102–122.

Steinhoff, Uwe. *On the Ethics of War and Terrorism*. Oxford, UK: Oxford University Press, 2007.

Steinhoff, Uwe. "Torture—The Case for Dirty Harry and Against Alan Dershowitz," (2006) *Journal of Applied Philosophy*, 23:3, 337–353.

Straub, Ervin. "Basic Human Needs, Altruism, and Aggression," in *The Social Psychology of Good and Evil*, ed. Arthur G. Miller. New York: The Guilford Press, 2005, 51–84.

Straub, Ervin. "The Psychology and Culture of Torture and Torturers," in *The Phenomenon of Torture*, ed. William F. Schulz. Philadelphia, PA: University of Pennsylvania Press, 2007, 204–209.

Straub, Ervin. *The Roots of Evil: the Origins of Genocide and Other Group Violence*. Cambridge: Cambridge University Press, 1989.

Strauss, David Levi. "Breakdown in the Gray Room: Recent Turns in the Image War," in *Abu Ghraib: The Politics of Torture*, ed. Anonymously with support of the Society for the Study of Native Arts and Sciences. Berkeley, CA: North Atlantic Books, 2004, 87–101.

Suedfeld, Peter. *Psychology and Torture*. London: Taylor & Francis, 1990.

Sullivan, Andrew. "The Abolition of Torture," in *Torture: A Collection*, ed. Sanford Levinson. New York: Oxford University Press, 2004, 317–328.

Sung, Chanterelle. "Torturing the Ticking Bomb Terrorist: An Analysis of Judicially Sanctioned Torture in the Context of Terrorism," (2003) *Boston College Third World Law Journal*, 23, 193–212.

Supreme Court of Israel. *Judgment Concerning the Legality of the General Security Service's Interrogation Methods*, in *Torture: A Collection*, ed. Sanford Levinson. New York: Oxford University Press, 2004, 165–182.

Sussaresses, Paul. "The Battle of the Casbah," in *The Phenomenon of Torture*, ed. William F. Schulz. Philadelphia, PA: University of Pennsylvania Press, 2007, 137–138.

Sussman, David. "What's Wrong With Torture?" (2005) *Philosophy and Public Affairs*, 33:1, 1–33.

Szántó, András (ed.). *What Orwell Didn't Know: Propaganda and the New Face of American Politics*. New York: Public Affairs, 2007.

Taft, William H. IV. "War Not Crime," in *The Torture Debate in America*, ed. Karen J. Greenberg. New York: Cambridge University Press, 2006, 223–228.

Tangney, June Price and Jeff Stuewig. "A Moral–Emotional Perspective on Evil Persons and Evil Deeds," in *The Social Psychology of Good and Evil*, ed. Arthur G. Miller. New York: The Guilford Press, 2005, 327–355.

Taylor, Stuart Jr. "The Skies Won't Be Safe until We Use Commonsense Profiling," in *Civil Liberties vs. National Security in a Post-9/11 World*, eds M. Darmer, B. Katherine, Robert M. Baird, and Stuart E. Rosenbaum. Amherst, NY: Prometheus Books, 2004, 157–162.

Thomson, Judith Jarvis. "A Defense of Abortion," (1971) *Philosophy & Public Affairs*, 1:1, Collected in *Ethics: History, Theory, and Contemporary Issues*, ed. Steven Cahn and Peter Markie. Oxford: Oxford University Press, 2002, 739–750.

Timerman, Hector. "Torture: A Family Affair," in *Torture: Does it Make Us Safer? Is It Ever OK? A Human Rights Perspective*, eds Kenneth Roth and Minky Worden. New York: The New Press and Human Rights Watch, 2005, 69–78.

Timerman, Jacobo. "Prisoner Without a Name, Cell Without a Number," in *The Phenomenon of Torture*, ed. William F. Schulz. Philadelphia, PA: University of Pennsylvania Press, 2007, 167–171.

Tindale, Christopher W. "The Logic of Torture: A Critical Examination," (1996) *Social Theory and Practice*, 22:3, 349–374.

Tindale, Christopher W. "Tragic Choices: Reaffirming Absolutes in the Torture Debate," (2005) *International Journal of Applied Philosophy*, 19:2, 209–222.

Tomaševski, Katarina. "Foreign Policy and Torture," in *An End to Torture: Strategies for Its Eradication*, ed. Dunér, Bertil. New York: St. Martin's Press, 1999, 183–202.

"Torture 1, Thematic issue focused on the 5th International Psychological Trauma Symposium," (2008) *Journal on Rehabilitation of Torture Victims and Prevention of Torture*, 18:1.

"Torture 3," (2007) *Journal on Rehabilitation of Torture Victims and Prevention of Torture*, 17:3.

Twining, William. "Bentham on Torture," (1973) *Northern Ireland Legal Quarterly*, 24:3, 305–357.

Twining, William and Paskins, Barrie. "Torture and Philosophy," (1978) *Aristotelian Society*, 52, 143–168.

US Department of Justice, Civil Rights Division. "Guidance Regarding the Use of Race by Federal Law Enforcement Agencies," in *Civil Liberties vs. National Security in a Post-9/11 World*, eds M. Darmer, B. Katherine, Robert M. Baird, and Stuart E. Rosenbaum. Amherst, NY: Prometheus Books, 2004, 175–188.

van der Veer, Guus. *Counselling and Therapy with Refugees and Victims of Trauma: Psychological Problems of Victims of War, Torture and Repression*. New York: Wiley, 1999.

Vidal-Naquet, Pierre. "Torture," in *The Phenomenon of Torture*, ed. William F. Schulz. Philadelphia, PA: University of Pennsylvania Press, 2007, 195.

Voltaire. "On Torture and Capital Punishment," in *The Phenomenon of Torture*, ed. William F. Schulz. Philadelphia, PA: University of Pennsylvania Press, 2007, 36–37.

Wall, Patrick. *Pain: The Science of Suffering*. New York: Columbia University Press, 2000.

Walzer, Michael. *Just and Unjust Wars: A Moral Argument with Historical Illustrations.* New York: Basic Books, 1977.

Walzer, Michael. "Political Action: The Problem of Dirty Hands," in *Torture: A Collection*, ed. Sanford Levinson. New York: Oxford University Press, 2004, 61–76.

Warner, Brooke. "Abu Ghraib and a New Generation of Soldiers," in *Abu Ghraib: The Politics of Torture* ed. Anonymously with support of the Society for the Study of Native Arts and Sciences, Berkeley, CA: North Atlantic Books, 2004, 71–86.

Weisberg, Richard H. "Loose Professionalism, or Why Lawyers Take the Lead on Torture," in *Torture: A Collection*, ed. Sanford Levinson. New York: Oxford University Press, 2004, 299–306.

Wenk-Ansohn, Mechthild. "The Vestige of Pain: Psychosomatic Disorders among Survivors of Torture," in *At the Side of Torture Survivors: Treating a Terrible Assault on Human Dignity*, eds Sep Graessner, M. D., Norbert Gurris, and Christian Pross, M. D. Baltimore, MD: Johns Hopkins University Press, 2001, 57–69.

Weschler, Lawrence. *A Miracle, A Universe: Settling Accounts with Torturers.* Chicago, IL: University of Chicago Press, 1990.

Westen, Drew. "The New Frontier: The Instruments of Emotion," in *What Orwell Didnz*

Wilson, John P. *Broken Spirits: The Treatment of Traumatized Asylum Seekers, Refugees, War and Torture Victims.* London: Routledge, 2004.

Wisnewski, J. Jeremy. "It's About Time: Defusing the Ticking Bomb Argument," (2008) *International Journal of Applied Philosophy*, 22:1, 103–116.

Wisnewski, J. Jeremy. "Unwarranted Torture Warrants: A Critique of the Dershowitz Proposal" (Summer 2008), *Journal of Social Philosophy,* XXXIX:2, 308–321.

Wisnewski, J. Jeremy. *Wittgenstein and Ethical Inquiry: A Defense of Ethics as Clarification.* London: Continuum, 2007.

Wisnewski, J. Jeremy and Henry Jacoby, "Failures of Sight: An Argument for Moral Perception," *American Philosophical Quarterly,* 2007, 44:3, 229–44.

Wittgenstein, Ludwig. *On Certainty*, eds G. E. M. Anscombe and G. H. von Wright. Trans. Denis Paul and G. E. M. Anscombe. New York: Harper & Row, 1972.

Wolfendale, Jessica. "Stoic Warriors and Stoic Torturers: The Moral Psychology of Military Torture," (2006) *South African Journal of Philosophy*, 25:1, 62–76.

Wolfendale, Jessica. *Torture and the Military Profession.* New York: Palgrave Macmillan, 2007.

Worden, Minky. "Torture Spoken Here: Ending Global Torture," in *Torture: Does it Make Us Safer? Is It Ever OK? A Human Rights Perspective*, eds Kenneth Roth and Minky Worden. New York: The New Press and Human Rights Watch, 2005, 79–105.

Wright, Jaime (trans.) *Torture in Brazil: A Shocking Report on the Pervasive Use of Torture by Brazilian Military Governments, 1964–1979*. New York: Random House, 1986.

Wu, Frank H. "Profiling in the Wake of September 11: The Precedent of the Japanese American Internment," in *Civil Liberties vs. National Security in a Post-9/11 World*, eds M. Darmer, B. Katherine, Robert M. Baird, and Stuart E. Rosenbaum. Amherst, NY: Prometheus Books, 2004, 147–156.

Yoo, John C. "A Crucial Look at Torture Law," in *Civil Liberties vs. National Security in a Post-9/11 World*, eds M. Darmer, B. Katherine, Robert M. Baird, and Stuart E. Rosenbaum. Amherst, NY: Prometheus Books, 2004, 321–324.

Zeeberg, Niels Steenstrup. "Torture—a Public Health Puzzle in Europe," (1998) *Torture Supplemental 1,* 25–44.

Zimbardo, Philip. "A Situationist Perspective on the Psychology of Evil: Understanding How Good People Are Transformed into Perpetrators," in *The Social Psychology of Good and Evil*, ed. Arthur G. Miller. New York: The Guilford Press, 2005, 21–50.

Zimbardo, Philip. *The Lucifer Effect: Understanding How Good People Turn Evil*. New York: Random House, 2007.

http://www.amnestyusa.org/denounce_torture/statement_on_interrogation.pdf (accessed July 5, 2008).

INDEX